SHEM FLEENOR

Ramparts Magazine's Vietnam War

1848 Publishing Company

New York City

ISBN: 9781951231-20-0

TABLE OF CONTENTS

INTRODUCTION

Page 3

CHAPTER ONE

"An Abstraction: The American War in Indochina"

Page 11

CHAPTER TWO

"Washington's War in Indochina"

Page 56

CHAPTER THREE

"The Corporations' War"

Page 80

CHAPTER FOUR

"Humanizing the War in Indochina"

Page 103

CHAPTER FIVE

"Bringing The War Home: The Antiwar Movement in America"

Page 139

EPILOGUE

Page 170

INTRODUCTION

Ramparts Magazine existed from 1962 –
1975. It was a glossy and often illustrated
American political muckraker that captured the
revolutionary zeitgeist of the era. Unlike most of
the radical magazines of its day, *Ramparts* was
expensively produced and stylistically
sophisticated. It was first established in June 1962
by Edward M. Keating in Menlo Park, California,
as a "showcase for the creative writer and as a
forum for the mature American Catholic." The
magazine declared its intent to publish fiction,
poetry, art, criticism and essays of distinction,
reflecting those "positive principles of the
Hellenic-Christian tradition which had shaped
and sustained western civilization for the
previous two thousand years," and which were,
Keating believed, still needed to "guide
American Catholics" in an age that had grown
increasingly "secular, bewildered, and afraid."[1]

---

[1] "Editorial Policy," *Ramparts*, vol. 1, no. 1 (June
1962), p. 3.

But under the editorship of Warren Hinckle, the magazine updated its look, became a monthly news magazine, and moved to San Francisco, California, which was an epicenter of the global counterculture. Robert Scheer became managing editor, and Dugald Stermer was hired as art director.[2] The trio proceeded to turn *Ramparts* into one of the best known and most respected organs of the American New Left.

The New Left can perhaps best be defined as a loosely organized, mostly white student movement that advocated democracy, civil rights, and various types of university reforms, and protested against the American war in Indochina. But the term New Left was first popularized in the United States in an open letter written in 1960 by sociologist C. Wright Mills titled *Letter to the New Left*. He argued for a new leftist ideology that he hoped might transcend

---

[2] Peter Richardson, *A Bomb in Every Issue: How the Short, Unruly Life of Ramparts Magazine Changed America*, (New York, The New Press, 2009).

the traditional and often dogmatic ("Old Left") focus on labor issues, into a broader focus on issues such as opposing alienation, anomie and authoritarianism. Mills argued for a shift from traditional leftism, toward the values of the counterculture, and, echoing Karl Marx, emphasized and advocated an international (rather than nationalistic) perspective on the movement. Mills also claimed that the proletariat (collectively the working-class referenced in Marxism) were no longer the revolutionary force; the new agents of revolutionary change were, he believed, young intellectuals (such as college students, scholars, and editors of leftist academic books, journals and muckraking publications such *Ramparts*).

Ramparts, perhaps more than any other publication of the era, was committed to being the conspicuous voice of the American New Left. But the magazine was also very much attuned to and committed to social movements around the world. Many articles published in *Ramparts* thus either mentioned, explicitly focused on, or published essays contributed to the magazine by several inspirations, influences, key figures, and luminaries of the New Left, including Albert Camus, Guy Debord, Allen Ginsberg, Emma Goldman, Che Guevara, Ho Chi Minh, Vladimir Lenin, Rosa Luxemburg, Herbert Marcuse, C. Wright Mills, Bertrand Russell, Jean-Paul Sartre, Leon Trotsky, Malcolm X, Mao Zedong, Mahatma Gandhi, Stokely Carmichael, Noam Chomsky, Angela Davis, Régis Debray, Tom Hayden, Abbie Hoffman, Huey Newton, Carl Oglesby, Jerry Rubin, Mario Savio, Bobby Seale, Todd Gitlin, Howard Zinn, and César Chávez. The pages of *Ramparts,* in short, read like a who's who of the New Left.

Despite its profound cultural significance, only one book by the second decade of the twenty-first century had been published about *Ramparts* – Peter Richardson's *A Bomb in Every Issue: How the Short, Unruly Life of Ramparts Magazine Changed America* (2009), which was awarded a *Mother Jones* Best Book of 2009 for its brilliant work uncovering the largely untold story of this great American muckraker. Richardson's book delved deep into the magazine's cultural significance and traced its trajectory from its 1962 birth as a "forum for the mature American Catholic" through its turbulent peak years (1967-1968), to its financially strapped demise in 1975. Richardson also deftly showed how that magazine shaped the counterculture in the Bay Area and vice versa. He also juxtaposed *Ramparts* against its contemporaries such as *Rolling Stone, Esquire,* and *Time,* and drew very useful connections to the later emergence of publications such as *Mother Jones.*

As magnificent and valuable as *A Bomb in Every Issue* is as an examination of the external life and times of the magazine and the men at helm of *Ramparts,* as a historian with a background in journalism I was more interested in the inner-life of magazine and its depiction and coverage of many of the most seminal events in world history during the 1960s and early 1970s. In other words, I was more interested in the magazine as journalistic history and the magazine's use as a primary source material that might provide historians with deeper insight into one of the most conflicted eras in American history.

Ramparts had been fully digitized online by the time I began researching and writing this three-part book series. The digitization of the magazine spanning thirteen of the most turbulent years in American and arguably world history provides academics with an amazing database of primary source material with which to get a great sense of how the American New Left narrated the events that shaped the Vietnam era in American history. The database and this trio of books about Ramparts offers a window into an America that does not exist anymore, namely a nation in which leftism was a viable political alternative and force that could have a profound impact on the polity. By September 11, 2001, there was no viable anti-war movement or rights revolution that was even remotely comparable to the movements championed in the pages of Ramparts. By then, both major political parties in the United States were unwavering proponents of American militarism as the cornerstone of American life and neither the Democratic or Republican political party had substantive programs designed to address the same racism, sexism, poverty, and degradation of the environment that were so central to the New Left's activism in the late-1960 and early 1970s. The militarism, corruption, warfare and corporate welfare that *Ramparts* routinely exposed had also not abated in the decades after the end of the Vietnam War and in many cases was far worse than it was than when *Ramparts* went out of business in 1975.

The book that follows is titled *Ramparts Magazine's Vietnam War,* which examines the publication's depiction of America's war in Indochina, which was a primary focus of the magazine's editorial staff. *Ramparts* published more essays about Vietnam than about any other single topic. The magazine also went out of business just a few months after the official end of the war. Chapters examine the magazine's depiction of Vietnam as several wars in one. Chapter One unpacks the magazine's depiction of the war as a cultural phenomenon and abstraction that happened 13,000 miles away from the continental Unites States. Chapter Two examines the magazine's depiction of corporate interests in America's war in Indochina, followed by a chapter that examines Washington's war in Vietnam. That chapter is followed by an examination of the war lived by American soldiers, as well as the war endured by the Vietnamese people. The final chapter examines *Ramparts Magazine's* unflinching advocacy of the antiwar movement in the U.S.

CHAPTER ONE

"An Abstraction: The American War in Indochina"

Ramparts Magazine was an early opponent of America's war in Indochina. The magazine's size and influence grew dramatically along with the scale of the war effort and the antiwar movement at home and abroad. Moving to monthly production, combined subscriptions and newsstand sales increased from just under 100,000 at the end of 1966 to nearly 250,000 in 1968, a figure more than double that of the liberal weekly, *The Nation*.[3]

One of *Ramparts Magazine's* most controversial covers depicted the hands of four of the publication's editors holding burning Draft cards, with their names clearly visible. Its April 1966 cover article also concerned the Michigan State University Group, a technical assistance program in South Vietnam that

---

[3] Dwight Garner, "Back When Ramparts Did the Storming," *The New York Times*, October 6, 2009.

Ramparts discovered was a front for CIA covert operations. For that story, *Ramparts* won the George Polk Award for Magazine Reporting.

In August 1966, managing editor James F. Colaianni wrote the first national article denouncing the U.S.'s use of napalm in Vietnam. "The Children of Vietnam," a January 1967 photo-essay contributed by William F. Pepper, depicted some of the heinous injuries inflicted on Vietnamese children by U.S. B-52 air strikes, which led Dr. Martin Luther King Jr. to oppose the war publicly for the first time.

The first overtly critical story published in *Ramparts* appeared in the July 1965 edition, eleven months after the Gulf of Tonkin incident rapidly escalated American involvement in Vietnam. *Ramparts* editors published a four-part series titled "Four Views on Southeast Asia." The first in the series was penned by *Ramparts* editor Robert Scheer. I was titled "A View From Phnom Penh." The second was an interview with Prince Norodom Sihanouk of Cambodia. It was titled

"A View From the Prince." The third was an essay contributed by a freelance international correspondent who had also written for *The Saturday Evening Post* and *Esquire* named William Worley. It was titled "A View From Djakarta." The fourth was titled "A View From Washington." It was written by Marcus Raskin, a former White House assistant under President John F. Kennedy. Raskin was, by the time his essay appeared in *Ramparts*, was a co-Director of the Institute for Policy Studies in Washington D.C.

Each article was critical of American involvement in Vietnam. Scheer, writing from the capital city of Cambodia where he had interviewed Prince Sihanouk, noted that the more entrenched America's war in Vietnam became, the more other Asian nations seemed to support Ho Chi Minh and Lê Duẩn's forces in the North, which was the antithesis of the Domino Theory rationale that American policymakers used to sell the war to the American public in the first place. Scheer, for example, quoted Sukarno, the president of Indonesia and former revolutionary leader against the Dutch, who said that the "nationalists" of the "New Emerging Nations" were aligned solidly alongside the National Liberation Front, the North Vietnamese and China in their "common resistance to American Imperialism!"[4] Prince Sihanouk, whose Cambodia offered sanctuary to the NLF and Viet Cong, had more immediate reasons to be weary deeper American involvement in Indochina. "Our hostility stems from the fact that the United States unconditionally supports the Vietnamese and Thais," he told Scheer, "not only against the Communists, but also against us, the Cambodians, who are neutralists and nationalists." The Vietnamese and Thais were the Khmer Realm's two traditional adversaries. "The day when the planes supplied by the United States (and piloted by Americans) no longer

---

[4] Robert Scheer, "Four Views on Southeast Asia. I. A View from Phnom Penh," *Ramparts Magazine*, July 1965, p. 31.

bomb our territory," Sihanouk explained, "when the American tanks, accompanied by South Vietnamese troops, directed by American advisors," no longer penetrated the Cambodian frontier villages carrying death, the day when America recalled her troops from Indochina, was the day when relations would inevitably relax between all parties involved in the conflict.[5]

Worley likewise prophesied that even if the United States were to have emerged from Vietnam a military victor that the nation would still ultimately lose politically, morally, and spiritually. "The cost in lives and treasure," he wrote, "the enmity of unborn generations will be wholly without recompense." For a brief while it would, he explained, "be possible to go on solemnly believing that grace and deity" were on the American side. But, he warned, America would be much wiser to heed Sukarno's warning

---

[5] Prince Sihanouk, "Four Views on Southeast Asia. II. A View from the Prince: Interview," *Ramparts Magazine*, July 1965, p. 33.

that "not even the gods in heaven" could "stop the flow of history!"[6]

Raskin rightly perceived American involvement in Vietnam to be closely associated to fears of China. Foreshadowing Nixon's détente with China less than a decade later, Raskin asserted that settlement of American war in Indochina could be used as an opening wedge for improving relations with Communist China.

In December 1965, *Ramparts* published an essay written by Bernard Fall titled "Vietnam Album." He cryptically explained that as long as the U.S. continued to fight the war, it would inevitably be losing the war. Even a total military or technological victory over the Viet Cong was going to be a partial defeat of American foreign policy goals — a defeat of the Americans by the Americans, as it were. Anticipating a very long war, he noted how extended occupations of

---

[6] William Worthy, "Four Views on Southeast Asia. III. A View from Djakarta," *Ramparts Magazine*, July 1965, p. 40.

colonies by empires had historically led to the toppling of those empires. The British, he wrote, had a 55-to-1 superiority in numbers of soldiers in Malaya and it took them thirteen years to win militarily, yet they still lost politically.[7] Fall lamented that the human element, which, he believed, had to be at the center of any deadly conflict, receded further and further into the periphery. Vietnam was simply a test case — on the American side of "credibility" in resisting Communist penetration; on the Viet Cong side it was, he asserted, a test of the possibility of changing the world balance by sidestepping the nuclear stalemate of the big powers. Or worse yet, he feared, Vietnam was simply a test bed of weapons and battle techniques. The armed peasant versus Detroit and the "think factories." But what Fall feared most was the creation of a more sinister and dehumanized societal ethics and banality of evil to match the increasingly

---

[7] Bernard B. Fall, "Vietnam Album," *Ramparts Magazine*, December 1965, p. 29.

mechanized and computerized warfare of the American empire.

In November 1966, *Ramparts* published an editorial titled "The Vietnam Elections." It was written by Marshall Windmiller, who had spent ten days in Saigon prior to the election interviewing politicians, Buddhist leaders, intellectuals, Catholics and students. Cynicism and contempt for the government was rife among these people and the overwhelming sentiments about the elections were that they were widely regarded as a farce. Indeed, in the National Assembly elections held September 27, 1963, just before the overthrow of the Diem regime, ninety-three percent of the voters supposedly voted, and Diem supposedly received ninety-nine percent of the popular vote. "Few American commentators," Windmiller wrote, "would now assert" that the fraudulent election represented "even an approximation of democracy." But with the announcement by the Saigon government that the voter turnout in the September 11, 1966 elections was almost eighty-one percent American government and journalistic opinion hailed it as a great step toward democracy. Despite a more plausible and believable voter turnout in 1966, South Vietnam's new constitution, Windmiller noted, had been rigged to insulate the nation's elites from the "threat of democracy."[8]

In December 1966, *Ramparts* published an article titled "Of Fish and Fishermen." It was written by Howard Zinn, who was a professor of Political Science at Boston University. Zinn noted that the only countries providing substantial aid to the American military efforts in Vietnam were Korea and Thailand, both of which were economically dependent on the U.S. under its military occupation, and controlled by oligarchs who could ignore popular desire. Zinn noted that Japan, which was also a station for American troops (under the much-resented Security Treaty of 1960) and its former territory, Okinawa, which

---

[8] Marshall Windmiller, "*The Vietnam Elections,*" *Ramparts Magazine*, November 1966, p. 4.

had been taken away by the U.S. and converted into one of the most powerful military bases in the world, made the Japanese citizens who he spoke to, many of whom had not forgotten to the U.S.'s dropping atomic bombs just twenty-one years earlier, feel uneasy about the prospects of another full-scale American War in the Pacific.

In May 1967, *Ramparts* published an essay written by Don Duncan titled "And Blessed be the Fruit." Duncan argued that the U.S. air bombing campaign in Vietnam equated to the United Nations charter's definition of genocide. The American people, he declared, "should know" what was "being done in their name."[9]

In February 1967, *Ramparts* published an essay titled "Saigon (*AP*) (*UPI*) Etc.: The Life & Times of the Vietnam Press Corps." It was written by an anonymous source who had spent eighteen months in Vietnam as an accredited reporter. The source described a political power structure that clearly wanted "the entire tradition

---

[9] Don Duncan, "And Blessed be the Fruit," *Ramparts Magazine*, May 1967, p. 31.

of a free press dismantled and the concept repealed."[10] The press was, the essayist explained, most often viewed with a mixture of contempt, scorn, or as potential public relations mouthpieces of official state department policies and prognostications. The source described a mostly intrepid Press Corps determined to do honest research and reporting to keep the public as well informed and part of the democratic process as possible. It was, the source asserted, bad enough the press personnel in Vietnam risked life and limb to fulfill what many perceived to be their duty as members of democratic societies, but the harassment, threats, and general climate of discord that existed between the military brass and policymakers posed a threat to a free and open society and seemed an omen of the American empire's descent into what the source perceived to be as fascism.

---

[10] Anonymous source, "Saigon (A.P.) (U.P.I.) Etc.: The Life & Times of the Vietnam Press Corps," *Ramparts Magazine*, February 1967, p. 46.

In July 1967, *Ramparts* published an article written by David Welch titled "Invasion Plans." Welch detailed rumors he had heard from a foreign national working at the American Embassy, from Western diplomats, from the Vientiane representative of the communist-led Pathet Lao, from a Thai government official, and from junior officers on General William Westmoreland's Saigon staff. The rumors were that the U.S. and Thai invasion of South Laos, where the Viet Cong were rumored to have a stockpile of weapons, was imminent. Ho Chi Minh's control of Laos enabled the NLF to construct the now famous trail named after him, which served as the main supply route for the NLF, the Viet Cong and the North Vietnamese Army. The rumored invasion of Laos, however, never quite materialized, perhaps in part because of Welch's article. The Ho Chi Minh Trail, however, stayed open for the entirety of the war and was essential to the North's eventual victory against the Americans and their puppet regime in the South.

Ramparts published another article written by Welch published in October 1967. It was titled "Pacification in Vietnam." As the Communist insurgency swept the Republic of Vietnam, one of Saigon's primary responses was a "pacification" program, which the French also tried to implement with disastrous consequences during that empire's occupation of Indochina a generation earlier. Along with the military effort to suppress the insurgency, the United States provided advice and support for the pacification effort, but for more than ten years that assistance was provided by a number of agencies without central coordination. To remedy this situation, American President Lyndon Johnson on May 9, 1967 directed the formation of an organization, to be composed of both civilian and military members, to provide American advice and support to the South Vietnamese pacification program. Welch discovered that America's pacification program was, much like the war itself, inspiring rather than preventing the spread of communism in Asia. America's "pacification" programs in Vietnam were also, he noted, terribly mismanaged and rife with corruption. Plus, the blatant violations of civil rights associated with the pacification program such as forcing farmers to move from their ancestral lands to live in "strategic hamlets" comparable to concentration camps provoked widespread rage and backlash in both the North and South of Vietnam.

In November 1967, *Ramparts* published an essay titled "The NLF's Program." It was written by Sol Stern. The NLF, Stern informed readers, demanded that if the U.S. unconditionally and permanently stopped the bombing of the North, the North would come to the conference table. Stern imagined the best-case scenario:

> Talks begin between the North and the U.S.
> These talks lead to a ceasefire in the South
> and a recognition of the Front by the U.S.
> The Front is then brought into the
> negotiations to deal directly with the U.S.
> on the question of withdrawal of U.S.
> troops. The withdrawal of North

Vietnamese troops could be tied to a staged
U.S. troop withdrawal from the South.[11]

Stern, however, lamented that his very sensible
best-case scenario for ending the war as
expediently as possible was considered
farfetched. "Unfortunately," he wrote, "many
Americans, even in the antiwar movement,"
continued to delude themselves about halfway
"compromise" solutions that would permit some
American presence to remain in Vietnam
indefinitely. It was, Stern snidely wrote, "as if the
American slaughter of the Vietnamese" had
given the U.S. some special prerogatives in that
country." The U.S was, he explained, an
occupying empire; the Vietnamese were,
conversely, fighting for their homeland. As such,
Stern concluded, withdrawal of all foreign troops
was the only reality the NLF was willing to
envision.[12]

---

[11] Sol Stern, "The NLF's Program," *Ramparts Magazine*, November 1967, p. 33.

[12] Ibid, p. 33.

In December 1967, *Ramparts* published an essay titled "The War Is Over." It was written by Jonathan Mirsky, who was a professor of Chinese Language and Literature at Dartmouth College. Mirsky had recently returned from Vietnam. "Both Vietnamese despair and American disillusionment lead to the final realization," he ominously wrote. "Nothing will come of all this. No country on earth has our supreme ability to obliterate."[13]

In June 1969, *Ramparts* published an essay titled "Talk, Talk; Fight, Fight." It was written by Tom Hayden, who had recently aided in the release of three American pilots from North Vietnam and three GIs from the NLF in South Vietnam. His article was especially interesting because he wrote from a moment in history when "Liberals" were "relaxing" and "radicals" were "drawing away" as a result of "the issue of peace" seeming to have been "accepted by most mainstream politicians." But the "feeling among

---

[13] Jonathan Mirsky, "The War Is Over," *Ramparts Magazine*, December 1967, p. 42.

antiwar activists that the Paris talks" signaled the end of the war could not, he warned, be more inaccurate. The Peace Movement, Hayden argued, needed to catch up with the worldwide feeling that the Viet Cong were the actual heroes of the war. This was the only position which, he concluded, was radically educational because it posed the possibility that "Americans should sometimes support communist-led revolutions."[14]

In August 1968, *Ramparts* published an essay titled "Open Arms, Closed Minds." It was written by Donald Duncan. He chronicled the rampant corruption in the South Vietnamese military. He, like Stern, underscored the determination of the Viet Cong, who were not, he explained, mercenaries fighting for money like the South Vietnamese regulars were, but for were in fact fighting for their independence from a foreign empire occupying its homeland.

---

[14] Tom Hayden, "Talk, Talk; Fight," *Ramparts Magazine*, June 29, 1968, p. 6.

In May 1969, *Ramparts* published an essay that began with an introduction from the editors. The essay was titled "Pacification in Viet-Nam: The Destruction of An Thinh." It was written by Roger Williams, who was a freelance correspondent, and accredited by the Department of Defense Press Service in Saigon. His article demonstrated that although the official nomenclature had changed, little else about the U.S.-led effort to pacify South Vietnam's hinterlands had changed. Corruption was still rife and bitterness amongst those who the South Vietnamese and the Americans hoped to pacify had not abated in the slightest. Williams' article, however, coincided with peace talks being held between the combatants in Paris. The end of the war, the State Department dishonestly asserted, was drawing near. The seemingly soon-to-be inevitable end of the war was, the State Department asserted, due to its accelerated pacification program in the hills and jungles surrounding Saigon and Khe Sanh. Williams' article, however, dissected and described that "search-and-destroy" missions were part and parcel of pacification, which, he argued, had "no lasting military effect on the NLF." The missions did, however, he warned, "produce millions of refugees bitter at the U.S. and thus eager to join the NLF. The Tet Offensive, he noted, made plain that the war was by no means anywhere near to being over. The Tet Offensive, in fact, forced American search-and-destroy units to fall back to protect urban enclaves, leaving the countryside to the NLF, which allowed them to move substantial numbers of large rockets to the very edges of the urban areas. With the NVA and Viet Cong seemingly on the offensive, U.S. Troops were increasingly spread thin, which further exacerbated the widespread lack of morale amongst the Americans that Duncan detected in his essay published in the October 1968 edition of *Ramparts*. "Positioning valuable combat troops hither and yon in villages having no direct military value," the editors concluded, "for dubious political advantages, was," they lamented, "reminiscent of the scattering of French troops prior to Dien Bien Phu." The siege of Khe Sanh in April 1968 also exposed the limits of America's seemingly unlimited firepower: despite saturation bombings, the Vietnamese were still able to bring directed fire on the U.S. airstrip, even in the final stages of the siege.[15]

In February 1970, *Ramparts* published an article titled "The Private War in Laos." It was written by Peter Dale Scott. The focus of the article was Madame Anna Chennault and her husband General Claire Chennault, who had fought in China with Chiang Kai-shek against Mao Zedong's forces in the late-1940s. After the war, General Chennault formed a private airline company. Both husband and wife had, through their involvement with the China Lobby and the CIA's complex of private corporations, played a profound role throughout American involvement in Southeast Asia. General

---

[15] *Ramparts* Editorial Staff, Introduction to Roger Williams "Pacification in Viet-Nam: *The Destruction of An Thinh,*" *Ramparts Magazine*, May 1969, p. 21.

Chennault's airline was, for example, employed by the U.S. government in 1954 to fly in support for the French at Dien Bien Phu. It was also a key factor in the new fighting which had begun in Laos in 1959; moreover, it appeared that President Eisenhower was not informed and did not know when his office and authority were being committed in the Laotian conflict, just as Nixon supposedly did not know of the intrigue of Madame Chennault soon before the 1968 election when the Democrats made an eleventh-hour bid for the presidency through a White House announcement that all bombing in North Vietnam was being stopped and that serious peace negotiations were about to begin. President Nguyễn Văn Thiệu of South Vietnam, who feared losing American support if peace talks were successful, publicly rejected the coming negotiations, which was a boon to Nixon, who had committed what Lyndon Johnson believed to be treason by colluding with Thiệu to win the election. Three days later, the Democratic candidate, Hubert

Humphrey, lost to Richard Nixon by one of the narrowest margins in American political history. In its evasion of Congressional and even Executive controls over military commitments in Laos and elsewhere, the CIA, Scott wrote, had long relied on the services of General Chennault's "private" paramilitary arm, Civil Air Transport (later known as Air America, Inc.).

In April 1970, *Ramparts* published a review essay titled "What the NLF Wants." It was written by Franz Schurmann, who was a Professor of History and Sociology at the University of California at Berkeley. Schurmann also wrote *Ideology and Organization in Communist China* (1968). He summarized Gabriel Kolko's edited publication of *Three Documents of the National Liberation Front*, which was a brochure published by Beacon Press in 1970. The brochure, which had never before been published in full in the United States, set forth the solution to the Vietnam War as proposed by the NLF and the Provisional Revolutionary Government of South Vietnam (PRG). The brochure forcefully stipulated that there would never be an end to the war until the Americans had left Indochina.

In June 1970, *Ramparts* published an article titled "The Vietnamization of Laos." It was written by Banning Garrett, who was affiliated with Pacific Studies Center as a specialist on Southeast Asia. The war in Vietnam and the war in Laos, Thailand and Cambodia were, he explained, "the same war."[16] They could not, he argued, as some U.S. prognosticators had naively (or deceptively) suggested, be fought or resolved in isolation from one another. In each of those nations the U.S. had armed, equipped and trained Asians to fight other Asians on behalf of the American empire's foreign policy directives. The U.S. had, he noted, consistently justified its actions in Indochina by saying that it was defending Laos and South Vietnam from North Vietnamese aggression. But this argument, Garrett asserted, had no more validity in respect to Laos than it did to South Vietnam. In short,

---

[16] Banning Garrett, "The Vietnamization of Laos," *Ramparts Magazine*, June 1970, p. 37.

while U.S. policymakers and mainstream media tended to ignore American intervention in parts of Indochina that were not also Vietnam, *Ramparts* conscientiously made the point of elaborating that the American empire was on the march in Southeast Asia, which was paid for most predominately with the blood of Indochinese people. "The Americans are willing," Garrett concluded, "to depopulate Laos: the Laotian people, on both sides and in the middle (an increasingly untenable position), are killing each other—and the Americans are pulling the strings."[17]

In February 1971, the editors of *Ramparts* published an essay titled "War Crimes." It was written by Frances Lang. He chronicled the testimony of some one hundred American veterans of the war in Indochina who had made public their own eyewitness accounts of war crimes committed by Americans in Vietnam. The National Committee for a Citizens' Commission

---

[17] Ibid, p. 45.

of Inquiry collected their statements on U.S. War Crimes in Vietnam, at what came to be known as the Winter Soldier Investigation. Many of the so called winter soldiers suggested that the official policy of the U.S. high command in Vietnam seemed to be genocidal and had thus turned American soldiers into murderers.

In May 1971, *Ramparts* published an article titled "The New Opium War." It was rritten by Frank Browning and Banning Garrett, with research assistance provided by Michael Aldrich, Adam Bennion, Joan Medlin, and Peter Scott. They conflated the increased repackaging of the Cold War into the Richard Nixon's nascent war on drugs. The ecology of narcotics had been, the essayists explained, disrupted and remade to coincide with the structure of America's Asia strategy — the stealthy conquest of a continent to serve the interests of the likes of the China Lobby (a group of American businessmen with interest in China). The shift in the international opium traffic was also, the authors argued, "a metaphor" for what had happened in Southeast Asia in the 1960s. As the U.S. had settled into Indochina after the French had mostly fled after Dien Bien Phu in 1954, its presence radiated a "nimbus of genocide and corruption," and "armadas of airplanes" that had come to "smash the land and lives of a helpless people."[18] The U.S. and boundaries reflecting the U.S.'s desires had been established, along with houses of commerce and petty criminality created in the American image that had, the essayists asserted, trained mercenary armies. One of the upshots of this process had been that the opium trade was systemically industrialized, given U.S. technological expertise and a shipping and transportation network as pervasive as the U.S. presence itself. The U.S. had — as a reflex of its warfare in Indochina — built up a support system for the trade in narcotics that was unparalleled in modem history. The U.S. thus went on what the essayists referred to as "a holy war" to stamp out

---

[18] Frank Browning and Banning Garrett, "The New Opium War," *Ramparts Magazine*, May 1971, p. 39.

communism and to protect its Asian markets and it "brought home heroin," which was, they believed, "a fitting trade-off" that characterized "the moral quality of the U.S. involvement." The essayists concluded the article by lamenting the deplorable heroin epidemic that seemed to be ravaging all segments, including affluent white America, in the early 1970s, which was, the essayists believed, "a tragic consequence" of the U.S.'s seemingly unwinnable and endless war in Indochina.[19]

In May 1972, *Ramparts* published an article written by Noam Chomsky titled "Indochina: The Next Phase." The article appeared in the magazine almost a year after the publication of *The Pentagon Papers*. *The Pentagon Papers* was a U.S. Department of Defense history of America's political and military involvement in Vietnam from 1945 to 1967. Daniel Ellsberg, who had worked on the study, released the papers to *The New York Times* in 1971. *The*

---

[19] Ibid, p. 39.

Pentagon Papers had demonstrated, among other things, that the numerous administrations who led the war effort had systematically misled or outright lied to Congress and the American public in order to sell the war. Chomsky wondered what, if any effect, this new knowledge would have in shaping the direction of the war. The release of *The Pentagon Papers*, in hindsight, seemed to have little effect on Nixon's handling of the war. It, however, came to light during the Watergate Investigation, that the Nixon administration broke into Ellsberg's psychiatrist's office in the hopes of finding information that could potentially harm Ellsberg and undermine the validity of the findings in *The Pentagon Papers.*

In July 1972, *Ramparts* published an essay titled "My Overthrown Resistance." It was contributed by Prince Norodom Sihanouk, the ex-Emperor of Cambodia. He continued to consider himself the head of that state during the French and Japanese occupation of Indochina. He was deposed in 1955 while visiting Moscow, and retired to the French Riviera soon after. He described the U.S. backed coup that removed him from power, which he believed had profound and lasting consequences in shaping America's all-but-inevitable and ill-fated war in Vietnam. In other words, he considered his toppling to have resulted in the U.S. quagmire in Vietnam and insinuated that his reinstallation could go a long way towards putting the proverbial genie back in the bottle.

In August 1973, *Ramparts* published an article titled "The Prospects of the Vietnam Offensive." It was written by Tom Hayden. He analyzed the nature and prospects of the Vietnamese offensive, and the basis for continuing optimism that the forces of the NLF expressed. He also proscribed ways in which the Democratic Republic of Vietnam could achieve a "just end" to their struggle against the American empire. He argued that the spring offensive in 1972 brought the generation-long war to its "most critical stage."[20] The war had reached a point in which the North Vietnamese forces were on the offensive and imposed "the conditions" under which they fought. Hayden noted that while the North Vietnamese were in Paris for peace talks and seemed particularly optimistic, the largest armada of B-52s in the history of aerial warfare was unleashing hundreds of thousands of tons of bombs on all of Vietnam. The American government and mass media were concomitantly declaring the North Vietnamese offensive to be "stalemated," "a last gasp," "a desperate attempt to shore up a negotiating position," and some were even proclaiming the North's imminent defeat.[21] The Nixon administration, like all American administrations since 1941, Hayden argued, found that its military technology was being used as a protective shield around an unsalvageable and hopelessly corrupt Saigon regime. The critical

---

[20] Tom Hayden, "The Prospects of the Vietnam Offensive," *Ramparts Magazine*, August 1972, p. 21.

[21] Ibid, p. 21.

nature of the crisis, Hayden explained, exposed by the spring offensive was that the Thieu regime could not stand on its own against withering and sustained revolutionary warfare. And since that regime and the Vietnamization program in general represented the last strategy seriously available to the American president, the time of final showdown in the Vietnam war seemed to have finally arrived.

In October 1972, *Ramparts* published an article titled "The Diplomacy of Terror: Behind the Decision to Bomb the Dikes." It was written by David Landau, who was the author of *Kissinger: The Uses of Power* (1972), which was the first major work to appear on President Nixon's national security advisor. Landau's article was based on secret diplomatic messages that were leaked to *Ramparts* editors. These leaks seemed to prove Hanoi's charge that the Nixon administration had systematically destroyed North Vietnam's dike system in bombing raids. "As Washington was well aware," Landau wrote, "the destruction of the dikes would cause the devastation of the North Vietnamese heartland and the slaughter of millions (of civilians) throughout the country." Landau, in short, saw the bombing of the dykes to be genocidal.[22]

In January 1973, *Ramparts* published a positive book review of Frances FitzGerald's *Fire in the Lake: The Vietnamese and the Americans in Vietnam* (1972). The review was written by Ngo Vinh Long, who was the Director of The Vietnam Research Center in Cambridge (England) and author of *Before the Revolution: The Vietnamese Peasants Under the French* (1973). *Fire in the Lake* was the first major book by an American on Vietnam, its history, and the U.S.'s intervention and war in Indochina. FitzGerald elaborated thousands of years of the history and culture of Vietnam, showing how that history affected the relations of its peoples with the relatively brief encounter with the Americans. FitzGerald and

---

[22] David Landau, "The Diplomacy of Terror: *Behind the Decision to Bomb the Dikes," Ramparts Magazine*, October 1972, p. 21.

Ngo agreed that the U.S. understood very little about Indochina and its leaders, and wrongly reacted to the threat of communism rather than recognizing the nation's long struggle to gain and keep its independence from foreign invaders. Ngo and FitzGerald agreed that American values of freedom, democracy, optimism, and technological progress were inconsistent with Vietnam's values, culture, and agrarian economy, making America's war in Vietnam a doomed effort from the start.

In March of 1973, *Ramparts* published another essay written by Landau titled "Peace is at Hand." In October of 1972, Henry Kissinger announced that Peace with honor seemed to be at hand. Five months later, Landau had yet to see any real peace in Vietnam. Violence had not, he noted, ceased and the U.S. had not withdrawn its military. "The President and Kissinger will bring not peace with honor but only escalation and endless war," he surmised. For despite all that had happened, the President and Kissinger would not, he asserted, hear of the fact that

Vietnam had exposed something very wrong and very ugly about American society; that the war's immense disruptive effect on the lives of the Vietnamese and of the U.S. could not be dismissed with a rapid diplomatic "sleight of hand." Nixon and Kissinger, he added, had not been alone in that failure; most Americans had shared in it as well.[23] Landau ominously portrayed the notion that peace was at hand by concluding that in spite of "manifold failures," the mainstream American press continued to "hail Kissinger as a diplomatic wizard." And while Vietnam stood at the brink of complete physical destruction, Americans, Landau concluded, still suffered "gladly the delusion" that American honor could be "salvaged from the wreckage."[24] The war, of course, dragged on for more than two more years. By then, Nixon,

---

[23] David Landau, "Peace Is at Hand," *Ramparts Magazine*, March 1973, p. 18.

[24] Ibid, p. 18.

cloaked in the dishonorable shame associated with Watergate, had resigned.

In April of 1973, *Ramparts* published another article by Chomsky titled "Endgame: The Tactics of Peace in Vietnam." He argued that the U.S. made agreements for peace, but almost immediately violated the agreements before the ink was dry on the documents. For example, The U.S. government announced that, in violation of the agreements it has just signed, it would continue to impose the regime it created on the people of the South, which was a violation of sovereignty according to the *UN Charter* (1948). In obvious defiance of the facts, President Thieu asserted that the agreements identified his government as the "lone legal government" in the South.[25] Washington agreed. Both were, however, Chomsky pointed out, wrong. He also cited a report made by Amnesty International, which discovered that many prisoners held in

---

[25] Noam Chomsky, "Endgame: The Tactics of Peace in Vietnam," *Ramparts Magazine*, April 1973, p. 27

the South were being abused and murdered, which also violated the peace agreement signed by the U.S. In short, even when peace seemed to be at hand, it was a rouse for the U.S. to wage more violence in Vietnam.

In July 1973, *Ramparts* published an essay titled "Cambodia: The War at the End of the Tunnel." It was written by Judith Coburn, who had made many trips to Cambodia as a journalist between 1970 and 1973. She also lived in Phnom Penh for a year as a reporter for the *Far Eastern Economic Review*. Cambodia, which bloodlessly negotiated its independence from France and managed to escape much of the Vietnam War, was by 1973 at the center of what she referred to as the next war in Indochina. She believed that the Khmer Rouge's violent ascendance over the previous decade was part-and-parcel of a "house of cards" the U.S. had unwittingly built in Indochina. From 1970 – 1973, the Khmer Rouge had been rapidly transformed from a small, isolated band of guerrillas into a formidable fighting force that controlled seventy-five percent of Cambodia's territory and forty percent of that nation's population. The Khmer Rouge had, in effect, Coburn wrote, "telescoped" two decades of the Vietnamese experience into three short years.[26] She argued that Sihanouk's return to power with a government considerably to the left of the earlier government the Americans found so inimical to their interests, seemed to be Cambodia's best and last chance for a peaceful future. Coburn, however, rightly believed that the Nixon administration would exploit Americans' growing lack of interest in Vietnam since peace seemed to at hand. After the Americans finally left Indochina in 1975, Cambodia sunk into a bitter war. In 1975, Pol Pot overthrew Lon Noi and Sihanouk became head of state, and the country was renamed Kampuchea. Thousands of residents of Cambodian cities were forcefully removed to country to become agricultural workers, currency became worthless, basic freedoms were

---

[26] Judith Coburn, "Cambodia: The War at the End of the Tunnel," *Ramparts Magazine*, July 1973, p. 42.

reduced, including the banning of religion. From 1975 – 1978, middle-class citizens were routinely tortured and often executed, many others starved to death or died from disease. The estimated death toll for this three year span was more than 1.7 million.

In January 1974, *Ramparts* published an essay titled "Vietnam: The Cease-Fire that Never Was." It was written by Ngo Vinh Long. War, Ngo argued, had not really abated, despite the assertions of the mainstream American Press, which was being spoon-fed information by the State Department. An average of one hundred South Vietnamese soldiers had been, he noted, killed or wounded every day in 1973 in the Mekong delta alone. The Mekong Delta was Vietnam's "rice basket" and thus heavily contested terrain. The endemic violence in the Mekong Delta meant less rice getting to Saigon, which led to widespread starvation, especially amongst the city's most indigent inhabitants, thousands of whom were war refugees from the hinterland. Thieu concomitantly launched an offensive in the Mekong Delta, which meant his army and bureaucracy consumed and stashed more rice as result. The most important reason for Thieu's increasingly aggressive military posture was the need for continued U.S. military and economic aid. His government also concomitantly exported rice in exchange for other material goods, which exacerbated the suffering of people in Khe Sanh and Saigon. It was, Ngo explained, a vicious cycle that seemed to exacerbate the fact that the war for survival that millions of Indochinese people had routinely suffered was far from being settled. Ngo thus cast Thieu as wasting more blood and treasure for no real reason but to slightly forestall his Titanic-like regime from sinking into the abyss of world history.

In July 1974, *Ramparts* published an extended essay titled "Report from Saigon: An Economy Near Collapse." It was written by William Shawcross, the author of *Dubcek and Czechoslovakia 1918–1968* (1970). Despite $700 million of USAID annually provided by

American taxpayers, South Vietnam's economy by no means resembled the South Korean or Taiwanese economies that American policymakers had promised it would. The decline in rice production described by Ngo above was central to the economic collapse described by Shawcross. In addition to the faux ceasefire that made the Mekong Delta (Vietnam's rice basket) a particularly dangerous warzone, corruption within the nepotistic Thieu regime, and failed attempts at privatization had ravaged the Vietnamese economy. In 1973, the money supply in South Vietnam increased by only nineteen percent against price increases of sixty-five percent. In this situation, demands by policemen and soldiers for bribes or food became more and more common and also, perhaps for the first time, impossible for ordinary people to meet, which further exacerbated violence. The communists were also routinely selling rice to villagers at a much lower price than Saigon could, which enabled the communists to more successfully win the stomachs and thus hearts and minds of the rural peasantry.

In April 1974, *Ramparts* published an article titled "Report in Saigon: Being Briefed." It was written by Danny Schechter, who was a News Director at *WBCN-FM* in Boston. Research for his article was partially paid for by a grant from the Fund for Investigative Journalism. Schechter put the rampant corruption of the Thieu regime into a larger context by conflating it with the evidence of rampant American political corruption which *The Pentagon Papers* and Watergate scandal especially underscored. Schechter also noted the pervasive corruption amongst public relations operatives at the American Embassy in Saigon and the American Press Corp. Reporters with another point of view from the state department, he wrote, were either denied access to Saigon (several were barred and others had been expelled in 1974) or found it impossible to gain access to official sources. Those that did successfully manage to get around the obstacles faced the prospect of government attempts to discredit them. That was what happened to Schechter. The article described his ordeal of being routinely railroaded by operatives at the American embassy, who often cajoled an Asia correspondent from the *Boston Globe* named Mathew Storin to denigrate him in print for traveling to North Vietnam to report on the war. Schechter assailed Storin as ostensibly being a "hack" for the state department and thus the worst kind of "journalist."[27]

In May 1975, less than a month after the American war in Indochina officially ended, *Ramparts* published three stories in a series titled "Vietnam Report." The first was titled "Why The Refugees?" written by Edward Block. He argued that the U.S. had as much of a moral obligation to get those who had aided the Americans out of Vietnam as the nation had of bringing home the American prisoners of war. It was, he argued, also a moral imperative that those American men

---

[27] Danny Schechter, "Report in Saigon: Being Briefed," *Ramparts Magazine*, April 1975, p. 16.

who were deemed "deserters" for "dodging" the Draft also be granted amnesty.

The second story in the series was titled "The Myth of the Hue Massacre." It was written by Edward S. Herman, who taught in the Wharton School at the University of Pennsylvania, and D. Gareth Porter, who was a co-director of the Indochina Resource Center. They argued that reports of the Viet Cong massacring "class enemies" on a "blacklist" during their brief 1968 occupation of Hue City during the Tet Offensive, which was reported by a United States Information Service (USIS) employee named Douglas Pike in 1970, was erroneous propaganda. Herman and Porter discovered that many civilians had in fact been killed, but most had died as a result of the Americans' indiscriminate use of violence when retaking the city. Much like Schechter in the April 1974 edition of *Ramparts*, Herman and Porter placed much of the blame for the pervasive and long-lasting misinformation regarding the so called "Hue Massacre" as a failure of the mainstream American media to adequately find and report facts, thereby making most of the American media little more than public relations agents for the State Department. Herman and Porter's consternation seemed to be both a commentary and a foreshadowing of the increased corporatization of the American mass media in the decades during and after America's war in Indochina.

The third and final essay in the series "Vietnam Report" was titled "Last Report From the Central Highlands." It was written by James Fenton, who traveled widely in Indochina. He was also a regular contributor to *The New Statesman* in London. Fenton described Saigon and South Vietnam as it succumbed to inevitable collapse as the Americans fled. He described great optimism amongst the victors. And though the North Vietnamese had finally won their war for independence against the French and then the American empires, history had, he explained, shown that the brand of capitalism that the

Americans in particular represented ultimately emerged as the victor.

Ramparts was at the proverbial frontlines of America's war in Indochina, serving as a muckraking watchdog that was a thorn in the side of the hawkish politicians and corporations that advocated the war and profited economically and politically from it. There was, however, not really one monolithic war in Vietnam. *Ramparts*, in fact, depicted several wars: Washington's War, the corporation's war, and the war experienced by working class Americans who were sent to Indochina, as well as the war suffered by Indochinese people who had been invaded, as well as the antiwar movement congealed with numerous other movements and the counterculture. *Ramparts*, as the chapters that follow help to illuminate, published scores of articles specifically focused on each of these facets and dynamics of America's war in Indochina.

CHAPTER TWO

"Washington's War in Indochina"

Ramparts Magazine published a handful of essays specifically focused on Washington's War in Vietnam. This chapter thus examines America's War in Indochina through the lens of the magazine's treatment and depiction of American foreign policymakers.

The first such essay published in *Ramparts* about the role of Washington insiders and operatives waging war was published in July 1965 in an editorial titled "The Unreasonable Question." *Ramparts* editors argued that public dissent on the war had been couched in supremely practical terms and questions, including: How was the U.S. going about the war? Should the nation be escalating or negotiating? Are American policies efficient? Was the U.S. winning the war? These were, the editors asserted, reasonable questions, asked by reasonable men. The unreasonable and "seemingly unutterable question" was, conversely, why was the U.S. in Indochina at all?[28] Why was, the editors asserted, the most essential query of all. But nobody in Washington seemed interested in pondering it. The editors concluded by asking readers: Why do serious, concrete, non-establishment proposals for peace stand so little chance of being heard and understood by American policymakers? Why — and this was to the editors the most disturbing question of all — was there no significant number of Americans asking these questions? Was the age of consensus that complete? Or, worse yet, had Americans lost all capacity for moral outrage?[29]

"The Unreasonable Question" was followed in the July 1965 edition of *Ramparts* by an article titled "The 'Vietnam Lobby.'" It was written by editors Warren Hinckle and Robert Scheer, who had recently completed an eighteen-month survey of Vietnam for the Center for the Study of Democratic Institutions. Scheer and

---

[28] *Ramparts* editorial staff, "The Unreasonable Question," *Ramparts Magazine*, July 1965, p. 15.

[29] Ibid, p. 15.

Hinkle presented a drawing of a dragon that represented the Vietnam Lobby. Joseph Kennedy was the head; Arthur Schlesinger was the tail. The Lobby was, Hinckle and Scheer argued, "an unusual alliance of ex-left intellectuals, conservative generals and liberal politicians." This collective's primary goal was to convince the public that "free Vietnam" was accomplishing miracles and could withstand the "Red onslaught" if the U.S. would just stop asking questions and continue to blindly support of the South's puppet regime.[30] Unlike the businessmen, missionaries, military personnel, and politicians that joined the China Lobby for self-seeking reasons, Scheer and Hinckle wrote, the members of the "Vietnam Lobby" were "True Believers" in a "Crusade for Democracy."[31] They collectively convinced the American public (including influential policymakers such as President Lyndon Johnson) that Ngo Dinh Diem

---

[30] Robert Scheer and Warren Hinckle, "Vietnam Lobby," *Ramparts Magazine*, July 1965, p. 20.

[31] Ibid, p. 24.

was a genuine proponent of democracy and that the best way to protect democracy around the world was to prevent the democratic process in Vietnam.

The "Vietnam Lobby" was followed in the July 1965 edition of *Ramparts* by an article titled "A View from Washington." It was written by Marcus Raskin, a co-Director of the Institute for Policy Studies in Washington D.C. He argued that what the U.S. did in South Vietnam would drastically influence Chinese activity. If the U.S., he asserted, helped in fashioning the political concerns of Southeast Asia on real issues — water, food, and electric power — the American empire would be far better positioned to blunt Chinese power because Indochina would have a rational reason for being independent from Chinese and Soviet influence.

In November 1965, fifteen months after the Gulf of Tonkin incident, *Ramparts* published an article titled "Proposals For a War Constitution." It was written by Arthur I. Waskow, who was a resident fellow at the

Institute For Policy Studies in Washington, D.C. Waskow described a document that had recently come into his possession. It was a proposal for a supposedly much-needed Constitutional reform championed by McGeorge Bundy that had been written for other high government officials, including President Lyndon Johnson. Bundy described the U.S. Constitution as "antiquated" because it only permitted Congress to declare war. He thus offered proposals designed to "salve" the public's "fears and soothe consciences without in fact interfering" with the government's "conduct and management of the war."[32] Bundy, in other words, detailed ways to mislead the American public so that Washington could wage its war unfettered from the qualms of the American people. He proposed adding "Article XXV" to the Constitution which would assert that "The Congress shall not have power to authorize in advance of the President to declare war on its behalf, except in the following

---

[32] Arthur I. Waskow, "Proposals For a War Constitution," *Ramparts Magazine*, November 1965, p. 42.

cases: (a) danger of thermonuclear war; (b) danger of escalated war; (c) danger of unjust war; (d) danger to vital interests of the United States; (e) danger to vital interests of the Free World."[33] Bundy's proposed article would thus remove the power to wage war out of the hands of Congress and put it under the jurisdiction of the President. It is important to note that this was authored by Bundy in reaction to the Gulf of Tonkin incident and Johnson's de facto declaration of war in which he had not officially declared war, which stoked special animus amongst antiwar advocates. Bundy's proposed article, in short, would retroactively make legal the law that Johnson had broken in 1964 when the president had ostensibly declared war on North Vietnam without first gaining the approval of Congress.

In December 1965, *Ramparts* published another essay written by Scheer titled "The Winner's War." The article detailed the rapid escalation of the American war in Viet-

---

[33] Ibid, p. 42.

particularly the centrality of relentless B-52 bombing raids (each plane carried fifteen tons of bombs) on North Vietnam, which began on June 18, 1965, and continued as an almost daily occurrence. "The New War of the Johnson Administration in Vietnam" Scheer wrote, represented a very sharp departure from the theory of counter-insurgency developed by the Kennedy brothers. The new turn was, Scheer argued, ostensibly "an attack" on the basic assumptions of Kennedy's foreign policy. Upon coming to power the Kennedy administration very quickly implemented the theories of counter-insurgency that up until 1965 had occupied a very vague and minority status within the military establishment. The basic concept, as applied to Vietnam, held that the Vietnamese would fight against the Communist guerrillas if the U.S. could convince them of the presumed and ultimately disastrous consequences of communism for their lives. It ʾs concomitantly believed to be essential that ʾ provided the counter-insurgents in

South Vietnam with the military know-how to withstand guerrilla warfare and the technical and economic knowledge to implement substantive reforms, which would make life in the areas controlled by the Government more attractive than under the rule of the communist guerrillas.[34] Johnson, conversely, adopted what he believed would win him a quick and decisive military victory by bombing Vietnam back into the Stone Age, and then worrying about political consequences of such carnage later. To Scheer, it seemed inevitable that the U.S. military would emerge from Vietnam victorious. He quite rightly feared that Johnson's apocalyptic bombing raids would create an impossible political situation for the Americans to solve.

In December 1966, *Ramparts* published an editorial titled "Presidential Papers." It was written by editor Marcus Raskin, who was in a unique position to observe the gradual changes in U.S. foreign policy that had led to the

---

[34] Robert Scheer, "The Winner's War," *Ramparts Magazine*, December 1965, p. 19.

country's involvement in Vietnam. Evidence, Raskin wrote, suggested that President Kennedy eventually recognized his mistake in sending additional troops in addition to advisors to Vietnam. In October 1963, Raskin explained, the White House issued a cryptic one-page statement soon after Secretary of Defense Robert McNamara returned from Vietnam. After stating that major assistance was needed only until the insurgency was suppressed, the statement went on to say that "Secretary McNamara and General Maxwell Taylor reported their judgment that the major part of the U.S. military task could be completed by the end of 1965, although there might be a continuing requirement for a limited number of U.S. training personnel in South Vietnam. They reported that by the end of 1963, the U.S. program for training the Vietnamese should have progressed to the point where only one thousand U.S. military personnel assigned to South Vietnam could be withdrawn. As Arthur Schlesinger later said, President Kennedy realized that he had made a bad judgment in

Vietnam and that the U.S. had to find an honorable way to extricate itself as quickly as possible.[35] Raskin concluded by stating that Americans had become "the new imperialists." The world knew, he asserted, that the U.S. could destroy Vietnam and China militarily, but they also saw that American souls needed "redeeming."[36]

In July 1967, *Ramparts* published another essay written by Raskin titled "America's Night of the Generals." He noted that it had recently become possible under the law for the Joint Chiefs to feel secure for four years in their jobs, and to lobby for the military's interest in Congress independent of the Secretary of Defense. The President also could not veto this legislation that was inspired by the Joint Chiefs, since the war had made him beholden to them. "During wartime the generals get what they

---

[35] Marcus Raskin, *"Presidential Papers,"* *Ramparts Magazine*, December 1966, p. 3.

[36] Ibid, p. 5.

want," Raskin wrote, "including domestic political power."[37] The article also illuminated the increased militarization of the American political system in the 1960s, and the increased power of the military at the center of the American experience.

The theme of the military commandeering the American polity was also a central theme of an article published in the August 1969 edition of *Ramparts* titled "Who the Hell Is Melvin Laird, Anyway?" The essay was written by Karl Hess, a former editor of *Newsweek*, the principal author of the 1960 Republican platform, a co-author of the 1964 platform, and Barry Goldwater's chief speechwriter. He took aim at Nixon's new Secretary of Defense, Melvin Laird, who had coined the expression "Vietnamization," referring to the process of transferring more responsibility for combat to the South Vietnamese forces. Hess described him as the

---

[37] Marcus Raskin, America's Night of the Generals," *Ramparts Magazine*, July 1967, p. 17.

"incarnation of institutional evil: the inevitable, historically predicted, institutional evil of delegated, non-participatory politics."[38] Laird was, Hess concluded, "no slavering Neanderthal fanatic of the right..." But he was a politician at the core of his being, which made him "reptilian." Laird would never dream of destroying the world, Hess wrote, "unless he were totally convinced that it made good sound political sense."[39]

In March 1970, *Ramparts* published an essay contributed by Bertrand Russell titled "On American Violence." He reminded readers that America was born of violence, noting the near genocide of Native Americans. Russell also noted that the U.S.'s use of the atomic bomb in order to emerge from World War II as the world's hegemonic imperial superpower. What was new in 1969 was, however, Russell wrote, that for the first time many affluent Americans were

---

[38] Karl Hess, "Who the Hell Is Melvin Laird, Anyway?" *Ramparts Magazine*, August 1969, p. 27.

[39] Ibid, p. 31.

"learning a very little of this disconcerting picture" as a result of the recent publication of Seymour Hersh's expose published in November 1969 about American solders wantonly murdering unarmed civilians in what came to be known as the My Lai Massacre.[40] Russell presciently declared that junior officers would be prosecuted for the heinous war crimes, but the "more wicked war criminals" were "the highest ranking military and civilian leaders, the architects of the whole genocidal policy." The whole establishment, he explained, "stood condemned," including those more moderate politicians whose every utterance was "dictated by caution and petty ambition..." The entire American people were, he argued, "now on trial.." If there was not a massive moral revulsion at what was being done in Americans' names to the people of Vietnam, Russell concluded, there was then little hope left for the future of America. Having lost the will to continue the

---

[40] Bertrand Russell, "On American Violence," *Ramparts Magazine*, March 1970, p. 55.

slaughter was not enough; it was, he concluded, imperative that the people of America repudiated their civil and military leaders.[41]

The upshot of My Lai was that William Calley was the only war criminal associated with My Lai, who was found guilty. He served three years under house arrest before his sentence was commuted by Richard Nixon. The vast majority of Americans agreed with the President's decision to absolve Calley and by implication the men who murdered hundreds of men, women, and children at My Lai, which seemed to underscore the moral corruption, turpitude, and lack of accountability central to the Americans' systemic slaughter of the Vietnamese people during the 1960s and 1970s.

In February 1971, *Ramparts* published an article titled "Vietnam: How Nixon Plans to Win the War." It was written by Banning Garrett, who noted that Kissinger, who he described as the "Strangelove" in the Nixon administration, seemed to be considering nuclear weapons,

---

[41] Ibid, p. 55.

particularly atomic landmines, as an expedient means of ending the war. "That the United States is now on the brink of using nuclear weapons in Vietnam is no more an occasion for wonder than that it has already crossed the threshold of systematic war crimes as defined by its own Nuremberg Tribunal," Garrett wrote. "Imperial war tends by nature to become genocidal war because it lacks the popular base and raison d'être of more conventional conflicts." And since, he wrote, the U.S. seemed powerless to win support among the Vietnamese and unable to garner the necessary troops from their own increasingly disaffected people, "the captains of the American empire must inevitably resort to ever more powerful technologies of destruction to stave off equally inevitable defeat."[42]

In December 1971, *Ramparts* published an essay titled "The Rise of Henry Kissinger." It was written by David Landau, who was the managing editor for *The Harvard Crimson*.

---

[42] Banning Garrett, Vietnam: How Nixon Plans to Win the War," *Ramparts Magazine*, February 1971, p. 31.

Landau argued that Kissinger, also a Harvard man, had yet to recognize that it would require little less than wholesale genocide to defeat Hanoi and the NLF in their native lands. He further noted that the regimes that Nixon and Kissinger sought to defend in Southeast Asia were among the cruelest and most totalitarian in the world. Their leaders imprisoned their political enemies, committed indiscriminate murder, and imposed a rule of terror and dictatorship on their native populations. And it was, Landau wrote, "not out of some perverted sense of fairness or democracy" that these regimes were being defended. It was "out of a harsh, brutal calculation of what an imperialist power like the United States must do to maintain itself in the world."[43] If smaller, more vulnerable men like Lieutenant William Calley, Landau concluded, could be sentenced for killing women and children in Vietnam (in the My Lai massacre), then there had to also be a higher

---

[43] David Landau, "The Rise of Henry Kissinger," *Ramparts Magazine*, December 1971, p. 44.

tribunal for statesmen like Kissinger, who upheld the policies which made such atrocities possible by playing his power game so well that his policy threatened to explode the very balance of forces which he had so ruthlessly defended.[44]

In February 1972, *Ramparts* published an article titled "Beyond the Pentagon Papers." It was written by Melvin Gurtov. He argued that the shape of Vietnam was dictated not by actual events and realities in Vietnam, such as the supposed threat of communist infiltration, but as a game of political football amongst Cold War rivals in Washington D.C. including Kennedy, Johnson, McNamara, Nixon, and Kissinger. All these men, Gurtov asserted, had hijacked the American polity and government, which led to the death and/or displacement of millions of Asians and tens of thousands of American lives for no real reason other than to aggrandize themselves and/or to save face, such as Kennedy after the Bay of Pigs debacle. Their arrogant, self-serving, and devastating miscalculations and

_____

[44] Ibid, p. 44.

mistakes had, Gurtov concluded, exposed elements of anti-democratic fascism deeply embedded in the American polity.

In April 1972, *Ramparts* published an essay written by Noam Chomsky titled "Nixon's Peace Offer." Chomsky wrote that the fundamental question central to the Indochina war had always been a relatively simple one; was the U.S. (or the French before it) to have a predominant voice in determining the political and social structure of Indochina, or would this question be settled by the Indochinese peoples themselves, relatively free from outside intervention? The conditions of U.S. intervention, Chomsky noted, had changed over the years, but not the essential goals and that the basic and glaring problem facing the "Western invaders" had also changed little during the previous quarter century. The U.S. had an enormous military force in the Pacific but little political power. Political violence was thus, Chomsky explained, inevitable.[45] The money spent on American militarization, in short, dictated American policy. In other words, American militarization was the tail that wagged the dog. Nixon's peace offer would thus be dictated by keeping the American military in Vietnam indefinitely. Even if Vietnamization were to prove to be a success, Chomsky argued, American weapons would continue to flow into the country and South Vietnam's Airbases would remain open to the American Air Force and Navy, whose Seventh Fleet was patrolling the South Pacific seas.

In August 1972, *Ramparts* published an essay titled "Nixon's Vietnam Strategy: How It Was Launched with the Aid of Brezhnev and Mao and How the Vietnamese Intend to Defeat It." This essay was penned by David Horowitz. The Vietnamese, he explained, intended to defeat what later became known as Kissinger and Nixon's "mad man thesis" by launching its own

---

[45] Noam Chomsky, "Nixon's Peace Offer," *Ramparts Magazine*, April 1972, p. 15.

offensive on the battlefield. This offensive was, Horowitz wrote, designed to undermine, militarily, the very pacification settlement that Nixon was preparing for the conference table at the next round of Peace Talks in Paris. Horowitz concluded by impugning the Soviet Union and China for "aiding" the Americans by not more explicitly supporting the NLF and DRV and Moscow and Beijing's "weakness in the face of Washington's campaign of terror" which, he asserted, "jeopardized the gains" that had been made "in the last decade toward putting some controls on the U.S. war machine." It was, he reminded readers, only the immense resistance put up first of all by the Vietnamese, but also by the American antiwar movement, that forced the issue of withdrawal to the center of the American political stage in the 1972 presidential campaign. "By dealing with Nixon in the hour of his escalations," Horowitz wrote, "the Russians and the Chinese undermined that effort, and thereby endangered world peace." He concluded by urging the American antiwar movement to vociferously defy the American and Soviet empires by following the "noble example of idealistic sacrifice established by the Vietnamese people."[46]

In November 1972, *Ramparts* published an article titled "McGovern and the Military." It was written by Richard F. Kaufman, who was an economist and counsel on the staff of the Joint Economic Committee of Congress, and author of *The War Profiteers* (1970). He argued that the ambitions and perquisites of warlords and bureau chiefs depended on the lavish use of public funds. The maintenance of unnecessary bases, the extravagant investment in military research and development, the procurement of "gold plated" weapon systems, the provocative and dangerous deployment of tactical nuclear devices, the continued buildup of strategic nuclear overkill capabilities, the fat logistical support tails that combat units lugged around,

---

[46] David Horowitz, "Nixon's Vietnam Strategy: How It Was Launched with the Aid of Brezhnev and Mao and How the Vietnamese Intend to Defeat It," *Ramparts Magazine*, August 1972, p. 20.

and the top-heavy officer corps were all, he explained, made possible by excessive defense spending. Fundamental reform of military policy could thus not, he noted, be attained without significant reductions in military spending.[47] George McGovern, Kaufman noted, was styled as the antiwar candidate and a would-be reformer of the military in the 1972 presidential campaign against Nixon, who was ambiguously styled as the "Peace With Honor" candidate. And though there was a vibrant and active antiwar movement in the U.S., the U.S. military ultimately dictated American foreign policy (as Chomsky argued) and also, as Kaufman argued, presidential politics. McGovern, the candidate more inclined to peace, was thus ultimately defeated in a historic landslide.

In January 1973, *Ramparts* published an essay written by Terry Pollack titled "Slow Leak in the Pentagon." Pollack chronicled a 23-year-old Air Force sergeant named Lonnie Franks

---

[47] Richard F. Kaufman, "McGovern and the Military," *Ramparts Magazine*, November 1972, p. 12.

who during the winter of 1971-1972, while working in intelligence, learned that U.S. planes had carried out scores of bombing missions over North Vietnam in direct violation of the rules of engagement such as they were at the time—and that Air Force personnel were routinely submitting false reports of these raids.[48] The article concluded with a call-to-action for would-be leakers and whistle blowers. "Once you have made the decision that you no longer can remain silent," Pollack wrote, "you ought to use your information in a way to maximize the impact." A well placed leak, he explained, had been known to halt a particularly objectionable government program, and, failing that, the revelation itself could go a long way in cracking excessive government secrecy and in changing popular beliefs. The article concluded by providing Brit Hume's contact information in Berkeley, California, as well as Jack Anderson and Seymour Hersh of *The New York Times* contact

---

[48] Terry Pollack, "Slow Leak in the Pentagon," *Ramparts Magazine*, January 1973, p. 22.

information for anyone interested in exposing government secrecy and corruption.

All told, *Ramparts* painted a very bleak picture of the warmakers in Washington that played such a central part in America's war in Indochina. *Ramparts* routinely depicted Washington's warmakers not as genuinely afraid of communism as a pernicious evil that needed to be eradicated, but as egomaniacal company men willing to openly and arrogantly lie to the American people in order to wage a genocidal war that served no real purpose other than to enrich the war profiteers who owned the American polity. As such, the next chapter focuses acutely on corporations' role in waging America's tragic war in Indochina.

CHAPTER THREE

"The Corporations' War"

Ramparts Magazine published several articles about corporations' centrality to America's war in Indochina. The war was big business and, many of the essays published by *Ramparts* suggested that capitalism was the root cause of America's imperial war in Vietnam. In December 1967, for example, *Ramparts* published an essay written by Don Duncan titled "Ordering Infernal Machines." Duncan detailed computerized weapons made by the likes of IBM that were used to kill civilians in Vietnam, such as the Guava cluster bomb, which could cut a human being to ribbons. Duncan's article presented engineers' renderings of some of the heinous devices designed to destroy. His essay particularly underscored the mechanized banality of evil at the root of the American militarization.

In February 1967, *Ramparts* published an article written by Sol Stern titled "The Defense Intellectuals." He focuses mostly on Herman

Kahn and Robert McNamara. Kahn was a founder of the Hudson Institute and one of the preeminent futurists of the latter part of the twentieth century. He originally came to prominence as a military strategist and systems theorist while employed at the RAND Corporation. He became known for analyzing the likely consequences of nuclear war and recommending ways to improve survivability, making him one of three historical inspirations for the title character of Stanley Kubrick's classic black comedy film satire that critiqued the nuclear arms race, *Dr. Strangelove* (1964). McNamara was a former President of The Ford Motor Company before becoming the eighth Secretary of Defense, serving from 1961 – 1968 under Presidents John F. Kennedy and Lyndon B. Johnson. McNamara played a major role in escalating the U.S.'s involvement in the war in Indochina. McNamara was responsible for the institution of systems analysis in public policy, which developed into the discipline known today as policy analysis. Both men, Stern argued, had created a newer and more banal style of warfare. Stern, however, rhetorically asked readers if Kahn and McNamara's methods had made society safer and healthier. "Does democracy have a better chance of surviving?" Stern queried.[49] It was no accident, he asserted, that the war in Vietnam had proven to be a "great blot" on McNamara's record, the one area in which his vaunted techniques had failed. They would, Stern concluded, continue to fail as long as he and his hired intellectuals continued to see Vietnam as merely a "problem" to be solved instead of recognizing it as a crisis in American ideology and values — a crisis which, Stern concluded, demanded that some hard questions be asked because decent values demanded them, and that some solutions be rejected not because they were invalid but because they were wrong.[50]

---

[49] Sol Stern, "The Defense Intellectuals," *Ramparts Magazine*, February 1967, p. 36.

[50] Ibid, p. 36.

The theme of America have being transformed into a corporatist and militarized state continued in the September 1969 edition of *Ramparts* in an essay titled "20,000 Guns Under the Sea." It was written by Seymour Hersh, the author of *Chemical and Biological Warfare: America's Hidden Arsenal* (1968). "The Navy and the weapons planners in the Pentagon," he wrote, had decided that much of "tomorrow's arms race" would be a "Jules Verne affair," and staged in the seventy-one percent of the world that was underwater.[51] The universities, through the Sea Grant program, were supplying the academicians to make modern warfare seafaring. The corporations, enticed by potentially immense profits, were, Hersh asserted, diverting research funds into the sea. The Navy, anxious to keep its share of the defense budget, was pushing its underwater missile systems. The prospects for stopping a juggernaut of these proportions were, Hersh concluded, "very dim." To do so would be

---

[51] Seymour Hersh, "20,000 Guns Under the Sea," *Ramparts Magazine*, September 1969, p. 40.

to change the processes by which the increasingly militarized American society was structured.[52]

In November 1969, *Ramparts* published an article contributed by Joseph Goulden and Marshall Singer titled "Dial-A-Bomb: AT&T and ABM," which elaborated that AT&T was the prime contractor and chief profit-maker for the highly controversial Anti-Ballistic Missile System, the ABM. The Nike-X Sentinel Safeguard ABM system was only the latest and most extravagant in a series of Nike defensive missiles that had garnered the telephone company nearly $10 billion in prime contracts since 1945. The top twenty-five U.S. defense contractors included, besides AT&T, such other stalwarts of the corporate aristocracy as Ford (which McNamara had left to wage war in Indochina), General Electric, General Motors and Standard Oil of New Jersey — the four largest industrial corporations in America. AT&T itself,

---

[52] Ibid, p. 44.

the largest American corporation of any kind, was a giant amongst giants. Its incredible assets of $40 billion (in 1969) approached the combined assets of America's fifty largest transportation companies (including airlines, railroads, etc.), or those of the three greatest industrial giants. Its net income was a third larger than that of the fifty largest U.S. commercial banks or of the fifty largest retailing companies combined. AT&T was also by 1969 the nation's sixth largest defense contractor, doing work on anti-submarine projects as well as the ABM. Yet AT&T's image was, Goulden and Singer wrote, "worlds away from the paraphernalia of war and devastation." The essayists thus rhetorically asked readers: what could be more pacific and tamer than the phone company?[53] It seemed no more likely a purveyor of nuclear missiles than did Macy's or the A&P. The story of demure Ma Bell's discreet but lucrative intimacy with the "defense

---

[53] Joseph Goulden and Marshall Singer, "Dial-A-Bomb: AT&T and ABM," *Ramparts Magazine*, November 1969, p. 29.

establishment" illuminated, Goulden and Singer asserted, much about the real nature of the military-industrial complex. But what, the essayists rhetorically asked, was the prevailing image of the military industrial complex? They explained that on the industrial side was a pack of "hustling upstart Texas yahoos and San Diego John Birch industrialists, inhabiting the new untamed wild west outlands of the American economy." On the military side were the "crackpot Strangelovean generals foisting their exorbitant arms-race war-games on an unwitting civilian society." But the reality was, Goulden and Singer argued, that the military-industrial complex was centered in the old respectable heartlands of corporate power, which had provided the basic impetus and thrust behind America's trillion-dollar "postwar war machine." The power of the complex was, they concluded, "clothed neither in brass and braid nor Bermuda shorts and a ten-gallon hat, but sensibly in a dark suit and a sober tie."[54]

---

[54] Ibid, p. 29.

In June of 1971, *Ramparts* published an article titled "A Reader's Guide to the Warfare State." It was written by Derek Shearer. He noted that despite Nixon's incessant double-speak related to transforming a wartime economy into a peacetime economy, his latest annual budget plan actually increased military spending by $6 billion in the following fiscal year alone. Also, in the two months spanning the end of 1970 to February 1971, shares of all aerospace companies climbed by an impressive 27.2 percent, compared with the 5.1 percent rise of all industrials listed in Standard and Poor's Index. General Dynamic's stock alone has risen 52 percent since January 1970, Litton was up an astounding ninety-five percent over its 1970 low, and McDonnell Douglas rose a staggering 111 percent from its 1970 low.[55] Investors, Shearer explained, understood keenly that the Nixon administration had shifted resources, not from military to

---

[55] Derek Shearer, "A Reader's Guide to the Warfare State," *Ramparts Magazine*, June 1971, p. 55.

human resources, but from military manpower to military hardware. But liberals in Congress, Shearer lamented, seemed "duped" into championing Nixon's supposed shift towards a peacetime economy, despite the fact that the January 23, 1971, issue of *The National Journal* listed thirty-six major weapons systems that would require almost $60 billion in additional funds in the coming years. Another one hundred weapons systems on which no accurate cost figures were available , Shearer rightly surmised, were likely to add billions more to the defense department budget.

In November 1971, *Ramparts* published an essay titled "The Strange Economics of the Vietnam War." It was written by Banning Garrett, who was a member of the Pacific Studies Center in Palo Alto, California. He discovered that the Japanese were especially anxious for an end to America's war in Indochina because they were excited about the prospect of gaining access to a new pool of highly disciplined laborers in postwar Vietnam. But foreign investors were leery of Article 22 in the South Vietnamese Constitution, which protected labor's right to organize. To ensure that this constitutional provision did not frighten off needed foreign (and for that matter domestic) investment, it should, Garrett noted, be made clear in the required implementing legislation that while labor had the right to organize and bargain collectively with management to influence management decisions, labor did not have the right of direct participation in those management decisions. *The Lillenthal Report*, which was researched and written before the Tet Offensive (January 1968) anticipated a swift U.S. military triumph and smooth establishment of a postwar economy that was friendly to American corporations. But that swift and decisive victory never materialized, which complicated the plans for a smooth postwar economic settlement, which were based on the assumption that the Americans would inevitably win the war. In late-1971, the Nixon administration promised a winding-down of the war. Garrett, however, like

Shearer, could read the proverbial tealeaves, which indicated that Nixon had no intention of winding down the war. "Quite the contrary," he wrote. Nixon's economic plan had revealed that Vietnamization was merely what Garrett referred to as the "latest scheme" in a historic gambit to safeguard existing political and economic stakes so that they would not have been made in vain. Nixon's quandary had thus become like that of the French before him: what the military had caused to be built. Shell and Caltex and sundry construction consortia would not, Garrett predicted, relinquish control; nor would the powerful men who gave Nixon his political existence permit him to give it up. After all, Garrett added, the waging of war brought forth the growth in Vietnam's capital plant, and recent political and military victories by the Vietnamese resistance had made it only too clear how difficult it would actually be to hold on to that investment without a military shield. And so once more, in a dance that seemed to know no finale, the plan to pacify the Vietnamese people through "economic development" proceeded apace, Garrett concluded, with the grim prospect of an even more brutal, armed, "protective reaction" lurking just beneath the surface.[56]

In November 1971, *Ramparts* published an essay titled "There's a Toyota in Their Future?" written by James Ridgeway. He noted that the U.S. had various economic game plans for post-war Vietnam. But as a practical matter Japanese businessmen, already active in South Vietnam, seemed more likely to influence the direction of economic development than American corporations and politicians. These Japanese businessmen, Ridgeway explained, seemed less interested in the vague regional plans advanced by the U.S. than in abundant supplies of cheap Vietnamese laborers who could be put to work making televisions and cars for sale in the U.S., Europe and Australia. In all likelihood, Ridgeway wrote, the Japanese would "become important trading partners for both North and

---

[56] Banning Garrett, "The Strange Economics of the Vietnam War," *Ramparts Magazine*, November 1971, p. 39.

South Vietnam; and thus their presence in the South in 1971 was more tenable than that of, say, American executives. The Japanese, he explained, could become the "vehicle for American investment."[57]

The U.S. had several studies for post-war economic development in Vietnam. The best known was the *Thuc-Lilienthal Report* (1969). It stated that the war actually helped South Vietnam because physical destruction was supposedly minimal and the economic wealth of the country had supposedly increased. As supposed proof, the report cited the network of airports, ports, and highways, all built by the U.S. military, and noted the rise of the army as a skilled labor force. Ridgeway, however, refuted such optimism, noting that agricultural development was likely not going to be possible on the wide-scale envisioned in the report because the U.S. military has poisoned the crop

---

[57] James Ridgeway, "There's a Toyota in Their Future?" *Ramparts Magazine*, November 1971, p. 40.

and forest lands. The rice markets were also glutted, and more intensive rice farming could lead to widespread unemployment.[58]

These facts did not, however, faze those such as Toyota, whose executives were eager to exploit post-war Vietnam by any means necessary. Both Japanese and American businessman eagerly envisioned Vietnam as a modern industrial economy, which was in stark contrast to the agrarian society it had been for thousands of years. South Vietnam's greatest asset, to companies such as Toyota, was not its agriculture, but its abundant supply of cheap, dependable workers. As a result, the scenario for post-war economic development seemed to look a lot like Cold War America's: the populace could be employed making goods for export in order to earn the foreign exchange to fuel and support the military state.

In November 1972, *Ramparts* published a collection of essays titled "*The RAND Papers.*" From 1964 – 1969 the RAND Corporation

---

[58] Ibid, p. 40.

conducted a major study of the National Liberation Front in Vietnam. Called the *Viet Cong Motivation and Morale Project*, this study gathered raw data from more than 2,000 interviews with NLF prisoners, defectors, and refugees captured in free-fire zones. The results of this study largely comprised what came to be known as *The RAND Papers*. *The RAND Papers* showed the hitherto unreported story of the key role which the *Viet Cong Motivation and Morale Project* played in the escalation of the war in 1965, and in the decision to commit massive numbers of U.S. air and land forces to Vietnam. *The RAND Papers*, however, wrongly depicted NLF morale as especially low and strongly implied that the impending collapse of the Vietnamese resistance was inevitable. And yet, *The RAND Papers* were at the core of Lyndon Johnson's war strategy. This report, the editors asserted, remained unavailable to congress and thus indicated yet another aspect of the erosion of the democratic decision-making process that had attended every phase of America's war in Indochina. The editors especially assailed Leon

Goure, the primary author of the article, because he distorted the evidence "in a manner that bordered on fraud" in order to justify the air war that the Pentagon wanted. The U.S. Air Force was also the chief financial supporter of RAND, and the editors noted this conflict of interest as being nothing short of criminal collusion that had cost millions of people their lives. The editorial concluded by elaborating that in November 1972 the U.S. Air Force had dropped 3,633,000 tons of bombs, or "a Hiroshima a week" for every week Nixon had been in office, which equated to billions of dollars in profits for weapons manufacturers.

The first full-length research essay that comprised *The RAND Papers* series published in the November 1972 edition of *Ramparts* was titled "Behind the Policy Makers: RAND and the Vietnam War." It was contributed by David Landau, the author of *Kissinger: The Uses of Power* (1972), the first major work to appear on President Nixon's national security advisor. Landau found the banality of evil described by

Hanna Arendt embedded in *The RAND Papers,* particularly the section titled "U.S. Responses to Enemy Escalation in Vietnam: A Checklist of Issues," which had been written by policy consultant Fred Iklé. Absent from Iklé's analysis, Landau lamented, was any evaluation of the soundness or humaneness of American policy in the war; gone was any mention of whatever anguish and destruction the war had caused. As had always been the case, there would be no trace of emotion; gone, even, was the perverse sense of excitement which American policymakers of an earlier generation had felt as they designed the scenario of escalation. Now, the options would be clicked off a checklist without embellishment much like one imagined a Nazi secretary ticking off the boxes next to the number tattooed into the skin a Jewish prisoner in a concentration camp. Part of the tragedy Iklé seemed to personify, in Landau's view, was "able intellectuals" prostituting "themselves and their talents" for a militarized society that valued victory and profits far more than the sanctity of human life. The greatest tragedy, however, in Landau's mind, was that Iklé and the other authors of *The RAND Papers* wrote about the war in negligible generalities that ignored the unique human qualities of the enemies of America's corporatist military. "It was a universal failure to grasp the unique nature of the insurgency in Vietnam," Landau wrote. The authors of *The RAND Papers* "just would not understand that the leaders in Hanoi, who had been regularly tricked in negotiations with the West, and the fighters in the South, who had little but contempt for the Saigon regime—and far more popular support—would not relinquish their goals either in negotiations or because of threats." For those who served at the RAND Corporation, Landau concluded, there could be little, if any, justification for self-sustaining delusions about the nature of the war.[59]

---

[59] David Landau, "Behind the Policy Makers: RAND and the Vietnam War," *Ramparts Magazine*, November 1972, p. 29.

Landau's essay was followed by an article titled "Looking Backward: RAND and Vietnam in Retrospect." It was written by Anthony Russo. "Body and spirit versus the bomb" was, he explained, what the Indochina war was "all about." In other words, he took a somewhat Luddite perspective that computers and machines had come to dictate the limits of human morality in times of war. RAND's analytics had failed, he explained, to make sense of the enemy's persistent morale in the face of what seemed to be certain defeat to a fairly more supplied and superior fighting force. In the mind of men like Iklé and McNamara, though many captured VC and NVA soldiers interviewed for the study professed to having high morale, it seemed impossible to the RAND analysts who thought in terms of resources rather than in terms of human nature and spirit. RAND analysts saw their captives and case studies in dehumanized terms rather than as determined revolutionaries willing to give their lives to defeat the seemingly vastly superior empire fighting a morally unjust war. Though Johnson was led to believe that North Vietnamese combatants' morale was very low and that the enemy was set to capitulate at any moment, RAND's files showed that North Vietnamese soldiers had actually maintained a surprisingly high level of morale throughout the war, a level of morale not equaled by the Nazi soldiers in World War II or the Chinese soldiers in the Korean War.[60] RAND analysts, in short, failed to understand that the Vietnamese were fighting for their land and families, in contrast to the Americans and South Vietnamese who were ostensibly mercenaries fighting because it was a job, rather than for moral reasons or ideological convictions.

The final article *Ramparts* published as part of *"The RAND Papers"* series was titled "War in the Back Pages." It was written by Tom Oliphant, who was a Washington correspondent

---

[60] Anthony Russo, "Looking Backward: RAND and Vietnam in Retrospect," *Ramparts Magazine*, November 1972, p. 42.

for *The Boston Globe*. The banality of American evil was also a central feature of Oliphant's article, especially his description of "the tonnage ritual." In the early days of the American war in Indochina, the American mass media often reported the "body count" of dead Americans and Vietnamese as if it was a football game and score was being kept. But by 1972 the American Air War was more often in the headlines than the dehumanized body counts that resulted from search-and-destroy missions. But nobody, Oliphant noted, ever mentioned just how much death and destruction was falling from American planes onto North Vietnam. Oliphant sardonically described the "tonnage ritual" as follows: The United States government did not tell the public what it was doing to Indochina from the air. All it did was add a number once a month to those already on file in the information office of the Pentagon, without in any way letting it be known that it was available to the public. As such, if no one bothered to call to get the figures it did not get reported. As it was, no national newspaper, no broadcast network, and no wire service sent out a story each month that began: "The United States and its allies dropped X thousand tons of bombs on Indochina last month."[61] Oliphant further elaborated that if he had not accidentally stumbled into a self-righteously naïve reaction to the tonnage ritual in January 1972, there would be no monthly record of the number at all in the public press. He thus indicted that the mainstream American Press was complicit in American War Crimes, rather than as serving as a check and balance on a corrupt and militaristic government that had waged an unwinnable war that cost millions of people their lives in order to enrich corporations, many of which were already conglomerated with American mass media outlets, such as *NBC, CBS* and *ABC*.

Rampart Magazine's depiction of corporations taking control of the American

---

[61] Tom Oliphant, "War in the Back Pages," *Ramparts Magazine*, November 1972, pp. 43.

polity and spearheading the militarization of American society and America's war in Indochina tended to speak in generalities and abstractions. In its attempt to expose the banality of evil deeply embedded in America's increasingly militarized and corporatist society *Ramparts* was also forced to present the war in largely dehumanized terms. However, contrary to popular historical memory propagated in movies such as *Forest Gump* (1994) that antiwar activists were unfairly unsympathetic to the American soldiers sent to Vietnam and often referred to them as "baby killers," *Ramparts* was, as the next chapter illuminates, actually very sympathetic to both American soldiers and the Vietnamese people. *Ramparts* tended to depict both American soldiers and the Vietnamese as victims of American corporations and politicians who were far more interested in power and the accumulation of wealth than the human cost and moral implications of Washington's and the corporations' war in Indochina.

CHAPTER FOUR

"Humanizing the War in Indochina"

The editorial staff at *Ramparts Magazine* made a great effort to humanize both American soldiers and Indochinese people, often portraying both to be the victims of the politicians and corporations who waged and profited from America's war in Vietnam. The first part of this chapter examines *Ramparts Magazine's* expressions of sympathy for and humanization of American soldiers. The second half examines the magazine's sympathetic and respectful humanization of the Vietnamese.

In February 1966, *Ramparts* published an essay titled "The whole thing was a lie!" It was written by Don Duncan, who was a master sergeant in the United States Army up until September of 1965. He retired after ten years of service, including six years in the Special Forces and eighteen months on active combat duty in Vietnam. He received the South Vietnamese Silver Star, the Combat Infantry Badge, the Bronze Star, and the United States Army Air

Medal. He was also nominated for the American Silver Star and was the first enlisted man in Vietnam to be nominated for the Legion of Merit. He participated in many missions behind enemy lines in War Zone D, Tung Tao and the An Khe Valley. In March 1965, he turned down the offer of a field commission to the rank of captain. He instead left Vietnam on September 5, 1965 and received his honorable discharge four days later. Duncan described himself as "a militant anti-Communist" when he joined the Army 1955 because, as he wrote, he "cherished democracy." But while in Vietnam he became painfully aware that he was not risking his life to protect and preserve Vietnamese democracy. He was, in fact, in Vietnam to spread anti-communism. He thus referred to young Americans who protested America's growing war in Indochina as "not against our boys in Vietnam." Antiwar activists were, he explained, actually opposed to Americans and Vietnamese people needlessly "dying for a lie, thereby corrupting the very word democracy."[62]

The theme of American soldiers going from gung-ho to against the American war in Vietnam continued in the July 1966 edition of *Ramparts,* which published another essay contributed by Duncan titled "Interview with Sgt. Smith." Duncan interviewed George E. Smith, who had been a staff sergeant in the Green Berets. Smith had been captured by the Viet Cong at Hip Hoa in November 1963, but was released in November 1965. Smith explained to Duncan that he had wanted to quit the Army in order to conduct a campaign to get the U.S. out of Vietnam. He asserted that that the U.S. had "nothing to gain from the war;" that the Viet Cong were the proverbial people; and that he was treated well when a captive, unlike prisoners of Saigon's troops; and that the U.S. could never defeat the Viet Cong, who believed they were

---

[62] Don Duncan, "The whole thing was a lie!" *Ramparts Magazine,* February 1966, p. 24.

fighting a war of Independence against an imperial and colonial power.[63]

In January 1967, *Ramparts* published an article titled "The War: Bubble Gum Soldiers." It was written by an anonymous Private First Class in the U.S. Army serving in Vietnam at the time the article was published. Shortly after he wrote this account of Fourth Infantry Division draftees facing combat duty in Vietnam, units of that Division suffered heavy casualties in fierce fighting near the Cambodian border. The essayist explained that a great many of the American soldiers who had fought in that fateful battle did not believe in the war they were risking their lives in. The widespread feeling of being exploited and imperiled to fight a "rich man's war" stoked especially ill feelings towards commanders amongst the men in the Division. The anonymous essayist was thus trapped in a catch-22: he felt as though he was risking his life and limbs to be part of the problem; but his

---

[63] Don Duncan, "Interview with Sgt. Smith," *Ramparts Magazine*, July 1966, p. 4.

refusal to risk his life and limbs fighting for the interests of corporations and the politicians could ruin his life and his family if he were to survive. He thus regrettably concluded his communiqué to *Ramparts* by explaining that all he could do to protest what he perceived to be an unjust slaughter of both the Vietnamese and young American boys from predominately working class families was to stick a piece of chewed gum on a picture of President Lyndon Johnson's face as a sign of protest.

In October 1967, *Ramparts* published an essay titled "The Deserters." It was written by Thomas R. Bransten. He wrote about a kind of underground railroad of antiwar activists who aided and abetted young American men who had been drafted to either hideout from authorities or to flee the country. The network often provided these so called "deserters," many of whom had families to support, temporary jobs, and housing.

In October 1968, *Ramparts* published another essay written by Duncan titled "Viet-

Name: The Decline and Fall of U.S. Morale." He revisited Vietnam after receiving several positive letters about an article he had previously written, which was critical of the war. As the title of the article rightly suggested, the morale of American soldiers went into steep and rapid decline in the months after the North Vietnamese Army's assault on Saigon in January1968, during the Tet Lunar New Year holiday. Many American GI's that Duncan spoke to could not understand why their lives were being put at risk for hazy or abstract objectives. The inability to locate the inherent justification for the war, which seemed increasingly unwinnable, even to *CBS's* Walter Cronkite, was the primary reason for a lack of morale deduced by Duncan and so many other pundits.

In September 1969, *Ramparts* published another article written by Duncan titled "The Prisoner" in which he chronicled Staff Sergeant George E. Smith's experiences as a prisoner of the National Liberation Front and then as a prisoner of the United States Army. After persistent inquiries as to their whereabouts, the U.S. military finally informed the press that Smith had been formally charged with giving aid to the enemy and would be tried in a court-martial in reaction to the statement he gave (see paragraph above pertaining to Duncan's interview with Smith from July 1966 edition) that some U.S. officials believed to be treasonous. Efforts to see Smith get him civilian counsel, and bring him back to the U.S. came to nothing as the months passed. Then, as quietly as he had been taken to Okinawa and as suddenly as the military had announced the court-martial charges, he was shipped to the U.S. and discharged—having been neither tried nor cleared of the charges which had been brought against him. In 1969, shortly after the North Vietnamese had seized the *USS Pueblo*, Smith contacted Duncan to tell his story of "harassment" at the hands of the U.S. Army. "To a person in San Francisco or New York," Duncan wrote, "the life George Smith led during this period may seem contradictory." He was antimilitary and resentful of the way the Army treated him, but he drew a disability pension (for leg wounds) and belonged to the VFW. He had, Duncan wrote, unwittingly become "part of the peace movement" whether he realized it or not.[64]

In February 1970, *Ramparts* published an article written by Peter Collier titled "Private Weise: Deserter." Collier seemed determined to inspire sympathy rather than derision amongst readers for those who had been drafted into the Armed forces to fight in an unjust war. Collier's essay chronicled the flight to Canada of David Weise, a young man who was compelled to live life on the run rather than go to Vietnam. Weise had crossed the U.S.-Canadian border at Vermont on Thanksgiving Day in 1968. By 1970, he had landed temporarily in Montreal where he worked with the American Deserters Cooperative. He could expect a minimum eight-year sentence if he dared return to the U.S.

---

[64] Donald Duncan, "The Prisoner," *Ramparts Magazine*, September 1969, p. 56.

Collier concluded by describing Weise as an idealistic hero who he hoped history would someday praise for his principled stance against an unlawful and amoral war.

Opponents of the antiwar movement often denigrated those who opposed the American war in Vietnam as naïve "peace-niks." They could not, however, so easily paint veterans of Vietnam who opposed the war with the same brush. In July of 1971, *Ramparts* published an essay written by Art Goldberg titled "Vietnam Vets: The Anti-War Army." Goldberg illuminated the central role the Vietnam Veterans Against the War had had assumed in the antiwar movement. Vietnam Veterans Against War began as a placard slogan in the staging area for the April 15, 1967 Spring Mobilization to End the War demonstration in New York City, in which 400,000 protesters participated. About twenty veterans of America's war in Vietnam gathered under that impromptu banner, including Jan Barry Crumb, who was a West Point dropout who had served in the war as a radio specialist in

an Army unit of a fixed-wing supply aircraft.
Following the conclusion of the march, Crumb
and five others formed the VVAW. Membership
passed 8,500 by January 1971, and thousands
more flocked to the organization after *Playboy
Magazine* donated a full-page VVAW ad in its
February 1971 edition, which also coincided with
the Winter Soldier hearings in which scores of
Veterans professed that they had witnessed
unreported and undocumented war crimes
committed by American soldiers in Vietnam. The
nationally televised coverage of the VVAW's
week-long April 1971 protest in Washington
D.C., which was the subject of Goldberg's essay,
and smaller protests in subsequent months
brought the organization even more attention
and members. An FBI informant who had
infiltrated the VVAW noted in March 1971 that
membership had grown from 1,500 to more than
12,000 in the previous four months. Goldberg
seemed surprised that so many members of the
VVAW were militantly nonviolent and seemed
to lament the increased militancy in the antiwar

and civil rights movements in contrast to the VVAW. "I don't think violence does any good," VVAW member Dennis Barden told Goldberg, "and I don't think blowing buildings up is right either." Nonviolence seemed to work better, he explained, because violence caused antiwar activists to hypocritically cede the moral high ground to the warmakers on Wall Street and Capitol Hill.[65]

In January 1973, *Ramparts* published an essay titled "Soldier: A Memoir." It was written by Anthony B. Herbert and James T. Wooten. The article began with an image of Lieutenant Colonel Anthony Herbert as he appeared on an Army recruitment poster. Winner of a battlefield commission, Lt. Col. Herbert was considered one of the very best combat infantrymen and commanders the American Army had ever produced. He had been trained in every military skill. He had engaged in clandestine, overt, and

---

[65] Art Goldberg, "Vietnam Vets: The Anti-War Army," *Ramparts Magazine*, July 1971, p. 17.

paramilitary operations and he seemed destined for a career that would lead him to the highest echelons of the Pentagon. But somehow, somewhere in Vietnam, Herbert's career took a dramatically different course. He thought he had been sent there to serve as a soldier. But in fact, he lamented, the situation demanded that he become something else—a murderer. Faced with the contradictions of his own idealism and the grotesque actualities of the war in Indochina, Herbert discovered that truth was more important to him than obedience and that he was more human than soldier. He thus became an outspoken opponent of American militarism.

Ramparts also published a number of articles that humanized the Vietnamese people. In November 1965, for example, the magazine published an essay titled "A Message of Singular Importance From the People of Vietnam." It was contributed by Robert S. Browne, an African-American official of a United States economic aid program who had lived for six years in Indochina — in Cambodia from 1955 to 1958, then in South Vietnam from 1958 to 1961. He had visited South Vietnam in the summer of 1965 and returned with a plea from the people that essentially contradicted what the Johnson administration represented as the desire of the South Vietnamese people for the U.S. to remain. "Not eager to see his country communized," Browne wrote, "the average Vietnamese would nevertheless greatly prefer this fate to a continuance of the unimaginable destruction" which Vietnam was "suffering." It was, Browne explained, the U.S., which felt that stopping communism or China was an objective that justified unlimited sacrifice. Most Vietnamese people, however, Browne explained, did not share this view. Essentially, the Vietnamese people who he spoke with wished that the Americans would go and fight their quarrels elsewhere. What was even more alarming to the Vietnamese than seeing the Americans push their country toward communism, Browne concluded, was seeing the Americans push Vietnam further into the clutches of China.[66]

In July 1966, *Ramparts* published an essay titled "Charlie's Long March." It was written by Jean Lacouture, the author of *Vietnam – Between Two Truces* (1966). He had extensive experience both as a diplomat and a reporter in Vietnam. In 1951, he joined the staff of *Le Monde*, first serving as head of the overseas bureau, and then as a reporter. He had also been diplomatic editor for *Combat* and the Cairo correspondent for *France-Soir*. In France, he taught at Institut d'étude du développement économique et social and was a Fellow for the Near Eastern Program at Harvard University. His essay was intended to humanize the enemies of American foreign policy directives in Indochina. He introduced readers to some North Vietnamese powerbrokers besides Ho Chi Minh, such as Nguyen Son, a top aide of Viet Minh General Giap. Lacouture also

---

[66] Robert S. Browne, A Message of Singular Importance From the People of Vietnam, *Ramparts Magazine*, November 1965, p. 2.

explained that at the time of the French's Custard-like defeat at Dien Bien Phu in 1954 that U.S. bombing raids had helped drive more Vietnamese people into the ranks of the VC. In other words, in its attempt to rid Vietnam of communism, American bombs actually inspired peasants to become communists. The long march of the "Viet Cong" was "not finished," he ominously wrote. And everything indicated that as long as the war lasted, the Vietnamese people would move more and more toward the left.[67]

In October 1966, *Ramparts* published another essay written by Lacouture titled "How to Talk to Mr. Ho." He provided a historiography of Ho Chi Minh's dealings with the French in the years after World War II, and then the Americans after Dien Bien Phu. The essay described both empire's failing to perceive Ho as a truly worthy adversary and their subsequent attempts to fool him. But Ho had, Lacouture explained, always been steadfast in his fight to rid his homeland of imperialists. Ho

---

[67] Ibid, p. 14.

would never, Lacouture explained, surrender until Washington solemnly agreed to self-determination in South Vietnam, and to the right of the NLF to play a role corresponding to its influence, and to the possibility of reunification, and when Washington announced it would evacuate Indochina, support neutralization, and show the seriousness of its intentions by concrete gestures such as cessation of bombing. Ho, Lacouture concluded, was nobody's fool and he would never surrender.

In January 1967, *Ramparts* published a series of essays titled "The Children of Vietnam." The first in the series was an editorial titled "A War Against Children" in which the editors of the magazine stated that the war in Vietnam had reached its ultimate and most barbarous stage, with the massiveness of American firepower being brought to bear in rural areas occupied largely by women and children. The statistics, the editors lamented, were "monstrous." Tens of thousands of Vietnamese children had been terribly burnt by American napalm and were receiving "scandalously inadequate" medical treatment. Many were also gradually dying as a result of wounds sustained by American firepower. A quarter million children had already died in what the editors called a "wasteful war," and another three-quarters of a million had been wounded or maimed since 1961. This destruction of children, the editors wrote, was not one of those sad but inescapable accidents of war. It was, they asserted, a direct and necessary result of the Johnson administration's policy of unrestricted and massive bombing of the Vietnamese countryside. This was, the editors lamented, a policy that, in the face of evidence presented in subsequent articles written by Dr. Benjamin Spock and William F. Pepper, made plain that the U.S. had a moral obligation to halt its bombing of Vietnam. There were, the editors concluded, certain issues beyond political considerations. The killing of children was one of them.[68]

---

[68] *Ramparts* editorial staff, "A War Against Children," *Ramparts Magazine*, January 1967, p. 10.

"A War Against Children" was followed in the January 1967 edition of *Ramparts* by Dr. Spock's famous preface to William F. Pepper's photographic essay, "The Children of Vietnam." Spock explained that more than one million children had perished in Vietnam during the U.S.'s occupation of the country. Those "lucky" to have survived often did not receive proper medical treatment. Those who did receive medical treatment often did so in dingy, dirty, rat and fly infested hospitals that sharply contrasted the incredible speed and efficiency with which American troops napalmed by mistake were given elaborate first aid while being lifted out of the battlefield and then flown to a Texas hospital for treatment. When Terre des Hommes, a Swiss humanitarian organization, asked for American government assistance in flying burned and wounded children to Europe for desperately needed treatment, American officials, Spock wrote, refused the request. A third of all Vietnamese children in institutions

---

had, Spock fumed, already lost both parents or been abandoned. He concluded his essay by asking readers: "Can America, which manufactures and delivers the efficient napalm that causes deep and deforming burns, deny all responsibility for their treatment?"[69]

Spock's essay was followed by "The Children of Vietnam: Photographs and Text." It was contributed by Pepper, who was an Executive Director of the Commission on Human Rights in New Rochelle, New York, a member of the faculty at Mercy College in Dobbs Ferry, New York, and the Director of that college's Children's Institute for Advanced Study and Research. On leave of absence in the spring of 1966, he spent six weeks in South Vietnam as an accredited journalist taking the nauseating pictures of maimed children published in the January 1967 edition of *Ramparts*. These images depicted children whose skin had been melted

---

[69] Dr. Benjamin Spock, "The Children of Vietnam, Preface," *Ramparts Magazine*, January 1967, p. 44.

by napalm, their sightless eyes, and limbs shattered almost beyond recognition. "What remained of their already shattered lives," Pepper wrote, "were ostensibly ruined." He noted that the rates of suicide had also skyrocketed by fifty percent in Vietnam, which was, he believed, was another tragic and unintended consequence of the American war. In several cases, group suicides that included children were reported in Saigon's newspapers. By waging war in Vietnam, the U.S. had, Pepper argued, "denied our own humanity, and descended more deeply than ever before as a nation, into the depths of barbarism." If ever a group of children in the history of man, anywhere in the world, had a moral claim for their childhood, he asserted, here they were in Vietnam. Every sickening, frightening scar, he declared, was "a silent cry to Americans" to begin to restore that childhood for those whom Americans were compelled to call their own because of what had been done in the name of America.[70]

In July 1967, *Ramparts* published another pictorial essay contributed by Lee Lockwood titled "The Face of the Enemy." It seemed a counterpart to Pepper's essay, which was published in January 1967. But rather than portraying Vietnamese children as helpless victims of American genocidal atrocities, it humanized the children of North Vietnam by showing them smiling warmly and without resentment.

In November 1969, *Ramparts* published an essay written by Franz Schurmann titled "Eulogy to Ho Chi Mihn," who died September 3, 1969, at the age of 79. Most American obituaries depicted Ho with veiled respect: as a nationalist, Ho was good; as a communist, he was bad. So it would appear that "Uncle Ho," as he was called all throughout Vietnam, was a split personality,

---

[70] William F. Pepper, "The Children of Vietnam: Photographs and Text," *Ramparts Magazine*, January 1967, p. 60.

agonizing constantly between good ends (nationalism) and bad means (communism). Ho was not, however, commonly viewed through such a dualistic lens in his homeland. For over half a century, Schurmann explained, Ho presided over the men and women who fought and planned for their country. "His manner was that of an old rural schoolteacher lecturing his pupils," Schurmann wrote. On a more cosmic plane, Ho was the leader of the only nation that had administered a major defeat to the U.S., the greatest empire the world had yet known. Nations and movements had leaders for three purposes, Schurmann explained: to lead them in the daily tasks of struggle, to unify men in the face of the conflicts which always arised to divide them, and to give them a vision of that for which they fought. A great leader was, Schurmann asserted, a commander, a conciliator, and a man of vision. Ho, the sixty years of his life as a revolutionary fighter, had all three capacities. From his earliest days in Paris, he took the lead in organizing groups of Vietnamese exiles; again and again he undertook dangerous political missions in Asia and Europe. In the midst of these revolutionary activities, he always managed at critical times to pull bitterly quarreling factions together into a new organizational unity. Ho's ability to unify moved the Vietnamese Revolution from the Indochinese Communist Party, to the Viet Minh, to the Democratic Republic of Vietnam. While Ho Chi Minh was not a theorist, he communicated to his people in simple terms a vision which was embodied in three words repeated again and again in every declaration by the Vietnamese: independence, unity, and sovereignty. "The meaning of these words," which Schurmann believed had lost much of their moral significance in America, was both the content of Ho's life and the spirit of the Vietnamese Revolution.[71]

In November 1970, *Ramparts* published another photo essay. It was titled "Children of

---

[71] Franz Schurmann, "Eulogy to Ho Chi Mihn," *Ramparts Magazine*, November 1969, p. 52.

Vietnam II" and contributed by French journalist Claude Johnes, who had collected drawings made by children who had survived American violence and atrocities. These drawings, which often depicted scenes of violence and carnage such as jets dropping bombs, and their brief, impressionistic thoughts on scenes from what had become daily life, showed that the violence of the war was subtle, grotesque, and irrevocably traumatic and scarring for the children that survived.

In January 1972, *Ramparts* published a story about a 16-year-old Vietnamese boy named Le Van Cau titled "Mascots of War." It was written by Jill Marti, a freelance journalist who had recently returned from a visit to Southeast Asia. La Van Cau began taking English language classes at the age of 13. By age 14, he had become a de facto interpreter between his elders and the American aid workers and military personnel. Over time, he developed cordial feelings with some American soldiers, who called him "Bobby." He was later recruited to be a "scout-interpreter." By age 16 he was being sent ahead on patrols and would relay to the Americans if certain people were VC, or harbored weapons. He eventually stepped on a land mine and lost his left leg and use of his right leg. Marti interviewed him while in hospital months after his accident. He expressed a great attitude, essentially stating that his American buddies – who had sent him ahead so as to diminish their own risk of injury – were good friends of his and he thus harbored no ill will towards them or any other Americans. Marti, however, exacerbated Le Van Cau's tragedy by noting a pocketful of pictures he had of his American buddies, most of whom had gone home to pursue education and jobs as he laid helplessly in a hospital in South Vietnam.

In October 1972, *Ramparts* published a eulogy titled "Nguyen Thai Binh, 1948-72." It was contributed by two forlorn and angry foreign students at the University of Washington who wished to remain anonymous. They had been comrades with Nguyen Thai Binh, whose name means "man of peace". Nguyen was a Vietnamese student who in 1968 was awarded a scholarship by the United States Agency for International Development (USAID). He attended Community College in California for a year before matriculating to the University of Washington, where he became active in the antiwar movement. February 10, 1972, he and nine students broke into and occupied the consulate of the Republic of Vietnam in New York City. They were arrested. Nguyen's student visa was revoked as a result of the arrest. Before returning home to Vietnam, Nguyen wrote two open letters to "lovers of peace and justice in the world" and another to President Richard Nixon criticizing actions he considered American crimes against the Vietnamese people. Seething over his expulsion from the University of Washington as well as the carpet-bombing of North Vietnam, Nguyen hijacked the Pan Am jetliner taking him back to Vietnam. Nguyen did not reveal his intentions to the crew until they were over the South China Sea. He passed a stewardess a note that read, "You are going to fly me to Hanoi and this airplane will be destroyed when we get there." When the flight's captain, Eugene Vaughn, refused to comply, Nguyen wrote a second note, which he splattered with his own blood. "This indicates how serious I am about being taken to Hanoi," it read. Vaughn went to the main cabin to meet Nguyen, who was a meek-looking young man who stood less than five feet tall. Nguyen showed off a foil-wrapped package that he said contained a bomb. Vaughn correctly guessed that the Nguyen was bluffing. The package actually contained lemons. Vaughn knew that one of his passengers, a retired San Francisco police officer, had come on board with a .357 Magnum. He discreetly told the ex-cop to be prepared to end Nguyen's life. Under the pretext of making a refueling stop, Vaughn landed at Saigon's Tan Son Nhat airport. Once the plane was at rest on the tarmac, Vaughn walked back to speak with the hijacker again. Nguyen was highly agitated, rambling about how he would detonate his bomb unless the plane left for Hanoi. "I can't understand you too well," said Vaughn. "Let me come closer." Nguyen leaned his head forward as Vaughn knelt down. Before Nguyen could repeat his demand, the captain grabbed him by the throat and thrust him to the floor. "Kill this son of a bitch!" Vaughn yelled as he pinned down the struggling Nguyen. The ex-cop came racing back with his weapon drawn and shot Nguyen five times at close range. Vaughn then heaved the hijacker's 116-pound corpse out of the Boeing 747's rear exit onto the tarmac. Many antiwar protestors in the U.S., including his anonymous comrades whose eulogy graced the pages of *Ramparts*, mourned his death and made him a symbol of the corruption, immorality, and lack of humanity associated America's war in Vietnam. Many conservatives, conversely, considered Vaughn a hero and a symbol of America's resolve.

In May 1973, *Ramparts* published an essay titled "The American POWs, Their Glory Is All Moonshine." It was written by Ngo Vinh Long, who was a director of the Vietnam Resource Center in Cambridge, Massachusetts. Ngo noted the jubilation associated with the recent release of American Prisoners of War, but underscored that the sense of humanity directed at the American POWs had been extended only to a rather select group of professional soldiers and civilian personnel, which was, he believed, in stark contrast to those Americans who bore the brunt of America's war in Vietnam, the veterans, who had been at best subjected to "benign neglect" after returning home. Moreover, the celebrations for the POWs had, Ngo believed, served to cover up and justify what he referred to as the "inhumane policies of the United States against the Indochinese people – the gooks, the dinks, the slant-eyes, the Oriental human beings." The television networks, he noted, indeed, paid almost as much attention to the dog brought back from Hanoi by a POW as they had to political prisoners who remained locked away in South Vietnamese prisons.[72] Reports from all over South Vietnam indicated that the government of Nguyen Van Thieu had embarked on a massive "reclassification" of political prisoners, moving them into the ranks of criminal offenders. Thus the thousands of jailed anti-Thieu politicians, intellectuals and students would be excluded in any mass release of political detainees once the war was officially ended.[73] Perhaps most regrettable of all, in Ngo's view, was that while the Nixon administration might have had abandoned all hope of retaining control of South Vietnam, it had not abandoned its goal of making South Vietnam a lesson and a warning to other countries in Southeast Asia, and possibly in Africa and Latin America. That lesson was that the price for opposing an American-supported regime was to be the "wanton destruction" of that country. If, by some miracle,

---

[72] Ngo Vinh Long, "The American POWs, Their Glory Is All Moonshine," *Ramparts Magazine*, May 1973, p. 11.

[73] Ibid, p. 14.

the rebellion was winning—as the Vietnamese people were winning – then the U.S. would, Ngo explained, sabotage attempts to reconstruct the country and carry out new programs.[74] Ngo's essay thus humanized both the American and Vietnamese soldiers concomitant to elaborating that the Nixon administration did not appear to humanize any of the combatants except the celebrated POWs, who were often used as a public relations campaign designed to cloak Nixon and Henry Kissinger in glory.

In December 1973, *Ramparts* published an essay titled "Vietnam: The POW's We Left Behind." It was written by **Fred Branfman**, who was the Director of the Indochina Resource Center in Washington, and the author of *Voices From the Plain of Jars: Life Under an Air War* (1972). He noted that Amnesty International estimated that by the end of 1973 South Vietnam had at least 100,000 political detainees, five times as many as the Soviet Union, Brazil, Greece and Turkey combined. But he also noted that such a

---

[74] Ibid, p. 13.

staggering figure tended to have a dehumanizing effect. He thus sought to redress the pervasive dehumanization of prisoners of war by telling the story of Nguyen Thi Man, a 22-year-old woman who had lost the use of her legs because she had been imprisoned in a Tiger Cage at Con Son Prison with four other women from 1969-1971. If the reader had ever seen the prisons in the movie *The Deer Hunter* (1978) he/she might get a better mental image of the misery Nguyen Thi Man suffered for two years in captivity. As the war was winding down, those left behind, such as "Bobby" and Nguyen Thi Man, faced an uncertain but probably heinous future after the Americans finally left Vietnam. She remained a political prisoner of the Republic of South Vietnam in December 1973 but, Branfman noted, there was little interest amongst American policymakers to "do anything" about political prisoners because Washington had grown so tired of the war and wanted to put the entire ordeal behind them. In Branfman's view, however, the U.S. had a moral obligation to ensure basic human rights to the 100,000 political prisoners that remained locked away and often tortured in South Vietnam's draconian prisons.

Also in December 1973, *Ramparts* published another photo-essay titled "The Rising Cry for Justice" that continued the theme of humanizing the Vietnamese. The photo-essay was comprised of serigraphs, paintings, and photographic silk-screens depicting mangled Vietnamese people, including scores of children, reminiscent of the 1890 slaughter of Lakota Sioux Indians at Wounded Knee. These graphic images illustrated "The Rising Cry for Justice," which was a room-sized exhibit on the Vietnam War created by students and faculty of the Immaculate Heart College Art Department in Los Angeles, California.

In May 1975, *Ramparts* published a report titled "Why The Refugees?" It was written by Edward Block, who had served during 1972-1973 as a refugee relief and rehabilitation officer in South Vietnam for USAID. Block laid the bulk of the blame for the millions of displaced

Vietnamese people on American bombers, which decimated both urban centers and rural farmlands, which created a refugee catastrophe all throughout Indochina. Much of the aid sent to provide relief to refugees in South Vietnam did not, however, get to those suffering due to rampant corruption. Much of the aid found its way to the military elites in the regime the U.S. backed, then often onto the black market. Corruption had grown so pervasive in South Vietnam by 1975 that Senators Edward Kennedy and Hubert Humphrey proposed legislation that would require any additional U.S. humanitarian aid appropriations earmarked for Indochina to be channeled through various multi-national agencies such as the International Red Cross, United Nations relief agencies, and private international relief organizations. "Only with measures such as these," Block wrote, could the Americans "insure against the continued political manipulation of refugees in South Vietnam," as well as to "prevent Saigon officials from adding more money to their already bulging Swiss bank accounts."[75]

Contrary to notions that antiwar activists on the New Left vilified American soldiers as "baby killers" and were overly sympathetic to the supposed enemies of American soldiers, *Ramparts* tended to be sympathetic to all of the combatants, depicting them as either proletariats or peasants who were victims of American corporations and politicians. Judging from the magazine's coverage of the combatants, it was not the warriors against which the New Left railed, but rather the war itself, which they depicted to be an atrocity that was a product of American imperialism and capitalist development. *Ramparts* was thus, as the next chapter helps to illuminate, fully committed to bringing the war home. That said, *Ramparts* most often advocated bringing the war home via peaceful means: protests, petitions, and by

---

[75] Edward Block, "Why the Refugees?" *Ramparts Magazine*, May 1975, p. 8.

shining a bright and glaring spotlight on the amorality of the American war in Indochina.

CHAPTER FIVE

"Bringing The War Home: The Antiwar Movement in America"

Ramparts Magazine was an unflinching advocate of the antiwar movement. The first of many such essays published in *Ramparts* was an editorial titled "Pax Americana." In it, the editorial staff of the magazine argued that the proverbial people of America, partly through "inertia" and partly through "wishful thinking" often blindly accepted the rhetoric, which presumed to prove that American military aggression was designed to preserve the security of the United States from communism. This was, however, the editors asserted, "palpably false." The Americans' "self-righteousness" that western civilization was the only true civilization was, the editors noted, comparable to Adolf's Hitler's Aryanism and the ancient Greeks' conceit that all non-Greeks were "barbarians." The notion that the U.S. would remake the postwar world in its own image spelled, the editors asserted, disaster for the entire world.

They also compared Vietnam, which the U.S. was "in the process of destroying," as an exercise and a testing ground similar to that of Spain in the 1930's, which had experienced a bitter civil war waged by fascists in an effort to topple democracy. "But more," the editors wrote, the U.S. empire's Asia policy was not dissimilar from its policies in Latin America, which, in spite of the Alliance for Progress, had further debilitated many of those countries, making them into what were ostensibly American colonies. "Africa is our sporting ground," the editors explained. "We use this vast continent much as we do ordinary peoples who are out of work and seeking jobs at whatever price."[76] The editors also described America as having the "power of the gods of Olympus," but also their weaknesses, too, most particularly hubris. The editors ominously concluded by informing readers that "once Rome was master of the world. Pax Romana. Rome fell to the barbarians. Once Nazi Germany, in its

---

[76] *Ramparts* editorial staff, "Pax Americana," *Ramparts Magazine*, December 1965, p. 3.

spasm of megalomania, threatened to master the world. Pax Germanica. A thousand years shrank to a miserly twelve. Now America was, they worried, "master of the world and tentative possessor of even the stars. Pax Americana."[77]

In July 1966, *Ramparts* published an op-ed written by Marcus Raskin titled "George Washington's Warning." The nation, which indulged toward another a habitual hatred, or a habitual fondness, was, Raskin paraphrased Washington, in some degree a slave. It was a slave to its animosity or to its affection, either of which was sufficient to lead it astray from its duty and interest.[78] While the French President Charles de Gaulle, in Raskin's mind, had effectively showed the Americans how a nation could carry on a foreign policy based on principles laid down by George Washington, American foreign policy concomitantly evinced

---

[77] Ibid, p. 4.

[78] Marcus Raskin, *"George Washington's Warning,"* *Ramparts Magazine*, July 1966, p. 6.

what kind of tragedy could befall a nation's political and economic elites when it was "carried away by cheap ideology and violence as its principal means of living in the world."[79] American national interest in Vietnam, Raskin concluded, demanded to be broader than the perpetuation of a corrupt military class, which the American taxpayer often unwittingly paid to keep in political power to fight a "holy war" against communism.

Ramparts brought the war home in August 1966 in an article titled "Napalm: A Small-town Diary," which was based on James F. Colaianni's experience as an opponent of a proposed plan to manufacture Napalm in Redwood City, California. He noted that opponents of Napalm being manufactured in Redwood City were deemed as "unpatriotic" by executives at United Technology Center (a subsidiary of United Aircraft). Colaianni and his cadre ultimately lost their fight to keep Redwood City from becoming

---

[79] Ibid, p. 6.

Napalm City USA. UTC had signed a contract with the Department of Defense to manufacture one hundred million pounds of Napalm. "On with the baby-roast," Colaianni snidely concluded his diary.[80]

In April 1967, *Ramparts* published an essay titled "Sanctuary." It was written by Donald Duncan about Draft resistors who had fled to Canada in 1966. No other institution outside of marriage, Duncan asserted, had influenced American society the way the Draft had. It had, he wrote, "perverted the purpose and the intellectual freedom of schools, and made military definitions of reality acceptable to society."[81] Through the Draft, he added, the military had also gained a subtle kind of control over the country, something it could never have achieved otherwise. "For the young men of our country," he concluded, "the military monkey will still be on their backs. For them, the great

---

[80] James F. Colaianni, "Napalm: A Smalltown Diary," *Ramparts Magazine*, August 1966, p. 50

[81] Ibid, p. 32.

debate (over whether to abolish, reform, of keep the Draft intact) would, he concluded, be like watching a TV instant replay: the outcome was known but everybody got another chance to see how it was done. And a few more of them, he promised, would inevitably leave for Canada.[82]

Ramparts published another article written by Duncan in May 1967 titled "And Blessed be the Fruit." The article began with the 1948 United Nations definition of genocide as: (a) Killing members of the group; (b) Causing serious bodily or mental harm to members of the group; (c) Deliberately inflicting on the group conditions of life calculated to bring about its physical destruction in whole or in part."[83] His article thus indicated that the U.S.'s B-52 bombing raids were genocidal, especially the use bombs such as Guavas, which dispersed razor sharp metal

---

[82] Ibid, p. 33.

[83] Don Duncan, "And Blessed be the Fruit," *Ramparts Magazine*, May 1967, p. 30.

fragments on impact and had been reported to have killed several civilians.[84]

Duncan's article in the May 1967 issue of *Ramparts* was followed by an essay titled "Declaration of Independence from the War in Vietnam." It was written by Martin Luther King Jr., based on an address he had presented at the Riverside Church in New York City on April 4, 1967. The speech was one of the first times King publicly opposed America's war in Vietnam, and he connected the plight of the Viet Cong to the plight of African Americans. "A nation that continues year after year to spend more money on military defense than on programs of social uplift is spiritually dead," he declared. King also provided five suggestions that he hoped might bring the war to a swift end. They were:

1. End all bombing in North and South Vietnam. 2. Declare a unilateral cease-fire in the hope that such action will create the atmosphere for negotiation. 3. Take

---

[84] Ibid, p. 31.

immediate steps to prevent other battlegrounds in Southeast Asia by curtailing our military buildup in Thailand and our interference in Laos. 4. Realistically accept the fact that the National Liberation Front has substantial support in South Vietnam and must thereby play a role in any meaningful negotiations and in any future Vietnam government. 5. Set a date on which we will remove all foreign troops from Vietnam in accordance with the 1954 Geneva Agreement.

King further noted that part of America's ongoing commitment would be to grant asylum to any Vietnamese who feared for his or her life under a new regime, which included the NLF. "Then," he asserted, "we must make what reparations we can for the damage we have done."[85] He concluded the essay by declaring that readers of *Ramparts* were living in

---

[85] Martin Luther King Jr., "Declaration of Independence from the War in Vietnam," *Ramparts Magazine*, May 1967, p. 36.

"revolutionary times" and that the "the shirtless and barefoot people of the land" were "rising up as never before." He called on readers to support these revolutions against imperial tyranny around the world, including in the cities of America. It was, he declared, a sad fact that, because of "comfort, complacency, a morbid fear of communism," Americans' "proneness to adjust to injustice, the Western nations that initiated so much of the revolutionary spirit of the modern world" had become the "arch anti-revolutionaries," and that many were increasingly driven to feel that Marxism was the truly revolutionary spirit. Americas only hope, King concluded, lied in the nation's ability to recapture the revolutionary spirit and go out into a sometimes hostile world declaring eternal hostility to poverty, racism, and militarism.[86]

King was murdered eleven months later. American civil rights remained an ongoing but largely ignored movement in the decades after

---

[86] Ibid, p. 37.

the end of the American war in Vietnam. American militarism and racism, however, had not much abated since the end of the Cold War. American military spending in the twenty-first century dwarfed what the empire spent on defense during the Cold War and the U.S. incarcerated more people, mostly African American people, than any other nation in the world, thereby undermining the U.S.'s claim of being a bastion of freedom. King's dream of true social justice and equality often seemed to many further from reach than it had when his essay was published in *Ramparts* in May of 1967.

In December 1967, *Ramparts* editors published an edition that included a picture of their hands holding their burning Draft cards on the cover of the magazine. They also published an editorial titled "Hell No, We Won't Go!" The war in Vietnam had to many Americans, "become so incredibly monstrous, its goals so undefined, its methods so horrible, its escalation so relentless, that the moral imperative to oppose it" had overbalanced the need for respectability;

and it also demanded "a break in life style."[87] When one subjected thirty million men to a totalitarian system (as evidenced by the Draft), even if it was American and indirect, the editors asserted, one had to expect a large portion of these thirty million men to rebel against that totalitarianism. The editors added that those who rebelled against the totalitarian's war in Vietnam were actually "behaving responsibly" in contrast to the genocidal maniacs in Washington who ordered Napalm to be dropped from B-52 bombers and who sent American men to search and destroy other human beings who were fighting a war for independence comparable to the war the Americans had fought against the British in the eighteenth century. The increased militancy of the antiwar protesters represented a genuine threat to the stability of society, the editors concluded, but that society's instability would be a pittance compared to the moral danger of the crime of silence which included

---

[87] *Ramparts* Editors, "Hell No, We Won't Go!" *Ramparts Magazine*, December 1967, pp. 31.

"mumbling on the sidelines" while the "war machine" moved inexorably on its way.[88]

The editorial published in the December 1967 edition of *Ramparts* was followed by a review of Norman Mailer's novel *Why Are We in Vietnam?* (1967) written by William M. Chace, who was an English professor at the University of California at Berkeley. Mailer's story followed a wealthy father who worked in the tobacco industry and his son as they went hunting for a Grizzly Bear in Alaska. As the novel progressed, the protagonist grew increasingly disillusioned that his father resorted to hunting tactics that seemed dishonest, including using a helicopter, to hunt the bear. At the end of the novel, the son informed the reader that he was soon going to fight for the Americans in their war against the Vietnamese. A major theme in Mailer's novel was the generational divide between the progressive youngster and his conformist and conservative father. The father was also a

---

[88] Ibid, p. 32.

metaphor for the conservative right's increased militarism and anti-communism in the decades after World War II and their dogmatic support of a genocidal war in Vietnam. The ideology of the conservative American was also especially illustrated through the characterization of Rusty and Tex Hyde. Rusty in particular was, like Mailer styled his public image to be, a hyper-masculine male who used the hunt to establish his dominance over other men and the wilderness. Mailer's characters ultimately fit into the allegory of the American empire's imperative to kill and show superiority over other countries, especially those supposedly moving towards communism.

In February 1968, *Ramparts* published an essay titled "The March on the Pentagon." It was written by Allen Woode, who had worked in the Pentagon during the October 21, 1967 protest of America's war in Vietnam, which led to famous images such as antiwar advocates gently placing flowers into the barrels of soldiers' guns. The article was essentially a tail of a man who paradoxically worked in the Pentagon but agreed with the antiwar protesters. He described the protests as a moral victory for the antiwar movement, but cautiously noted that a moral victory equated to a loss. He suggested coordinating 30,000 phone calls to the Pentagon, which, he noted, would do far more to occupy those who worked in the Defense Department than 300,000 dissidents on the lawn ever could.

In March 1968, *Ramparts* published an essay titled "The Regrouping of Doves." It was written by Peter Dale Scott, who was an assistant professor of English at the University of California at Berkeley, and a co-author of *The Politics of Escalation in Vietnam* (1966). The chances of peace between 1954 and 1968, he asserted, had been consistently frustrated by selective and then strategic escalations of the war. Together, they had the effect of defining, by deeds more loudly than words, a U.S. rejection of meaningful peace objectives. Peace would mean, Scott believed, a political catastrophe for President Johnson because the Communist Party was the one truly national organization that permeated both North and South Vietnam; it was also the only group not dependent on foreign bayonets for survival. Escalation was thus necessary to preserve what Scott referred to as the "corrupt Saigon 'Republic,'" which was essentially a cadre of wealthy military families comparable to feudal lords. And as the determination of the Viet Cong forces became more and more apparent, Scott concluded, so did that of America's hawks on Capitol Hill and Wall Street for a wider war. Only a comparable escalation by the American antiwar movement, he explained, could prevent the most recent calls for an end to the bombing — and a Geneva solution — from being "drowned again in the noise of a still wider war."[89]

In June 1969, *Ramparts* published an essay titled "Uncovering the Nerve Gas Coverup." It was written by Seymour Hersh, who was the

---

[89] Peter Dale Scott, "The Regrouping of Doves," *Ramparts Magazine*, March 1968, p. 58.

author of *Chemical and Biological Warfare:
America's Hidden Arsenal* (1968). Since its
founding in 1941, Hersh explained, much of the
activity at Dugway Proving Ground in Utah had
been a closely guarded secret. Activities at
Dugway included aerial nerve agent testing of
chemicals that caused one's respiratory system to
go into a state of paralysis and suffocate its
victims to death. On March 13, 1968, the
scientists at Dugway test-fired a
chemical artillery shell containing one hundred
and sixty gallons of nerve agent in an open air pit
and a jet aircraft sprayed nerve agent in a target
area about 27 miles west of Skull Valley. Six
thousand sheep on ranches surrounding the
valley were killed in the incident. The Army tried
to cover up the incident because, as Hersh wrote,
it had "all the elements" for a nationwide
scandal: target practice with a lethal nerve agent,
an incredibly obvious series of military lies, a
heavy concentration of newspaper and radio-
television reporters, and a national presidential
campaign. But, Hersh puzzled, the sheep deaths

led neither to congressional outcries about the
military's Chemical Biological Weapons
program, nor to a public debate about such
weapons; nor did it even provoke any serious
citizen reaction in Utah, which was one of the
more conservative states in the nation. Concern,
from the highest levels of state officialdom on
down, was that too much investigating or talking
about the incident might make the Army move
its CBW base from Dugway. "The nerve gas
incident was perhaps more terrifying but really
no different from other mistakes, or accidents, or
decisions at military bases all over the nation,"
Hersh concluded. Lying became the order of the
day and the prevailing attitude was "don't rock
the boat" because Pentagon funds brought not
only goods and services to Dugway and other
parts of the Sunbelt, but also the "cooperation
and zeal" of countless men on Capitol Hill, in
federal agencies in Washington, and in state
capitals from Maine to Hawaii.[90]

---

[90] Seymour Hersh, "Uncovering the Nerve Gas
Coverup," *Ramparts Magazine*, June 1969, p. 14.

In June 1969, *Ramparts* published an article written by Peter Collier titled "The Passion of Tommy Smothers." The essay hailed the comedian, who was also an outspoken critic of America's war in Vietnam concomitant to denigrating corrupt powerbrokers that controlled American industries. Tommy Smothers and his brother's variety show, *The Smothers Brothers Comedy Hour*, became one of the most controversial American TV programs of the Vietnam War era. Despite popular success, the brothers' penchant for material that was critical of the political mainstream and sympathetic to the counterculture led to their ousting by *CBS* executives in 1969. The network even spitefully refused to air the show's final episode. Collier's article was thus especially critical of *CBS*, which he depicted to be a metaphor of the conservative nature of American mass media, which he believed had systemically failed in its duty to truthfully report facts to the American polity all through the Vietnam War.

In July 1969, *Ramparts* published a photographic essay contributed by Jeffrey Blankfort titled "Our Town: The War Comes to Beallsville." The essay profiled five families in an Ohio town with a population of just 450 inhabitants that had lost five sons in Vietnam. The general sentiment in Beallsville, at least amongst those interviewed by Blankfort, was that the war was decimating an entire generation of young men for no good reason and should thus be stopped with all due haste. The war, however, dragged for nearly six more years.

In August 1969, *Ramparts* published an article titled "The NLF Asks the American Left: Where Are You?" It was written by Franz Schurmann, who was a professor of history and sociology at the University of California at Berkeley. Schurmann noted that as the global antiwar movement seemed to being catching a second wind, many American antiwar activists seemed to be increasingly tuning out. "No matter how tired Americans may have become of the war," he urged readers, exhaustion paled in comparison to the war ragged Vietnamese in both the North and South.

In December 1969, *Ramparts* published an editorial titled "The Viet-Nam Moratorium." The Moratorium to End the War in Vietnam was a massive demonstration that included numerous teach-ins across the nation against the U.S.'s involvement in the Vietnam War. The Moratorium took place on October 15, 1969, followed a month later by a large Moratorium March on Washington D.C. *Ramparts* editors agreed that America's war in Vietnam had to end as quickly as possible. They, however, pointed out that the war was actually a symptom of American imperialism and capitalism. In other words, there needed to be, the editors asserted, a moratorium on American imperialism and capitalism or America's militarized society and endless warfare would never wither away and would only grow more entrenched. The job of the radicals in the Moratorium was, the editors explained, to convince the new protesters that Vietnam was no simple aberration, but rather the natural outgrowth of a social and economic system that sought to lock the third world into a permanent state of indentured servitude. "Changing the system," the editors wrote, had to first mean the "liquidation of the global empire" that had "grown to such mammoth proportions" since the end of World War II.[91] If that empire was not dissolved, then withdrawal from Vietnam, they warned, merely meant cutting losses in one war to save energy for a newer quagmire (such as the War on Drugs and War on Terror). The editors concluded the essay by lamenting that no major political figure of either party had felt compelled to call for a complete withdrawal from imperialism in the months after the highly publicized Moratorium. But, they asserted, a withdrawal from imperialism was the real key to peace in Vietnam. If the resources of the underdeveloped world were not left to those nations to control and develop, the editors ominously predicted, and if the U.S. military arm

---

[91] *Ramparts* editorial staff, "The Viet-Nam Moratorium," *Ramparts Magazine*, December 1969, p. 9.

was not withdrawn — not only from Southeast Asia, but from all of Asia, Africa and Latin America — then the U.S. was inevitably and inexorably destined to "walk down the already visible path of national suicide, and even perhaps global annihilation."[92]

In August 1970, *Ramparts* published an essay titled "Jocks 1, War 0." It was written by Jack Scott. Scores of college athletes had, Scott explained, joined the student movement, not as fellow travelers temporarily caught up in the emotional momentum of antiwar activity, but as committed strugglers alongside their fellow students. Scott described the Cal Berkeley athletic department as one of the last bastions of conservatism in the half-decade after the Free Speech Movement, which began in earnest in 1964 outside Sproul Hall. In May 1970, Scott noted, Cal's campus witnessed massive riots. Some student-activists even went to class and demanded that the discussion be of the

---

[92] Ibid, p. 9.

American invasion of Cambodia. The Cal regents feared more intensive riots and ultimately closed the university for a four-day weekend. Many athletes took part in the Cal uprisings, as well as the Columbia and Paris student protests in 1968. Scott noted that they were also surely inspired by the Tommie Smith and John Carlos's iconic Black Power salute on the medal podium at the 1968 Olympic Games in Mexico City.

In April 1971, *Ramparts* published an essay titled "People's Peace Treaty." It was written by the editorial staff of the magazine. The Joint Treaty of Peace Between the U.S. and Vietnamese Peoples was signed in Hanoi by North and South Vietnamese students and an American delegation led by David Ifshin, who was president of the National Student Association. The treaty listed the following terms to end the war as expediently as possible:

1. The Americans agree to immediate and total withdrawal from Vietnam and publicly to set the date by which all

American forces will be removed. The Vietnamese pledge that as soon as the U.S. government publicly sets a date for total withdrawal:

2. They will enter discussions to secure the release of all American prisoners, including pilots captured while bombing North Vietnam.

3. There will be an immediate cease-fire between U.S. forces and those led by the Provisional Revolutionary Government of South Vietnam.

4. They will enter discussions of the procedures to guarantee the safety of all withdrawing troops.

5. The Americans pledge to end the imposition of Thieu-Ky-Khiem on the people of South Vietnam in order to insure

their right to self-determination and so that all political prisoners can be released.

6. The Vietnamese pledge to form a provisional coalition government to organize democratic elections. All parties agree to respect the results of elections in which all South Vietnamese can participate freely without the presence of any foreign troops.

7. The South Vietnamese pledge to enter discussion of procedures to guarantee the safety and political freedom of those South Vietnamese who have collaborated with the U.S. or with the U.S.-supported regime.

8. The Americans and Vietnamese agree to respect the independence, peace and neutrality of Laos and Cambodia in accord with the 1954 and 1962 Geneva conventions and not to interfere in the internal affairs of these two countries.

9. Upon these points of agreement, we pledge to end the war and resolve all other questions in the spirit of self-determination and mutual respect for the independence and political freedom of the people of Vietnam and the United States. By ratifying the agreement, we pledge to take whatever actions are appropriate to implement the terms of this joint Treaty and to insure its acceptance by the government of the United States.[93]

The editors asserted that the Vietnam War, which superior technology and geographical immunity seemed to insure would devastate only the victims, had become "a grotesque liability to the executioners as well."[94] They lamented that despite a rhetoric of de-escalation, the Nixon administration had in fact deepened

---

[93] *Ramparts* editorial staff, "People's Peace Treaty," *Ramparts Magazine*, April 1971, p. 13.

[94] Ibid, p. 14.

the war into Cambodia and Laos. Meanwhile on the home front the chaos grew to a crescendo — rising inflation and unemployment, open assaults on civil rights and other gains of the previous decades, and a growing wave of political violence and repression from above, all of which seemed to make evident to the editors of *Ramparts* that the destinies of the people of Vietnam and the citizens of America had become inextricably linked.

In July 1971, *Ramparts* published an essay written by Michael P. Lerner, who was a member of the militant antiwar organization known as the "May Day Tribe." His essay was titled "May Day: Anatomy of the Movement." The 1971 May Day Protests were, he explained, a series of large-scale acts of civil disobedience in Washington D.C. in protest against the Vietnam War. The protests began on May 1 of that year and continued with similar intensity into the morning of May 3rd, then rapidly diminished through several following days. Members of the Nixon administration believed the events to be damaging, because the government's response led to mass arrests and were widely perceived as violating citizens' civil rights. Thirteen thousand antiwar protestors had been arrested in less than a week, and the nation's capital had been all but paralyzed. The energies which had languished in the year since the Kent State massacre in 1970 were again aroused, Lerner wrote, and the use of mass civil disobedience without anyone getting killed presaged the development of a political force that could conceivably bring the war closer to an end. Conspiracy charges against May Day Tribe leaders were levied but soon dismissed. And most of the thirteen thousand demonstrators arrested were released without charges (seventy-nine were eventually convicted). The ACLU pursued a class action suit brought by thousands of detained protesters and ultimately the U.S. Congress, recognizing the illegal nature of the arrests, agreed to pay a settlement to those arrested, making them some of the only citizens in U.S. history to receive financial compensation for violation of the constitutional right of free assembly.

In April 1975, *Ramparts* published a review written by Andrew Kopkind of Bert Schneider, Richard Pearce, and Peter Davies' Academy Award winning-documentary *Hearts and Minds,* the title of which was based on a quote from President Lyndon Johnson who famously said the ultimate victory in Vietnam would depend on winning the hearts and minds the Vietnamese people. Kopkind wrote that the recently released documentary confronted the consequences of what he referred to as the "war-within-the-war." Kopkind described the filmmakers' methodology as both didactic and evocative. *Hearts and Minds,* Kopkind argued, was designed to summon anger, love, rage, disgust, bitterness, and joy.[95] He felt that one of the strongest aspects of the film was the way in which the filmmakers exacerbated cultural

---

[95] Andrew Kopkind, "*Hearts and Minds*: The Adamant Memory of Vietnam," *Ramparts Magazine,* April 1975, p. 40.

differences between bourgeois American materialism and the revolutionary peasants of Vietnam who were the first fighting force to ever beat the Americans militarily. The film premiered at the 1974 Cannes Film Festival. But Commercial distribution was delayed in the United States due to legal issues, including a temporary restraining order obtained by one of the interviewees, former National Security Advisor Walt Rostow, who claimed that the film was "somewhat misleading" and that he had not been given the opportunity to approve the results of his interview before the film was published. Columbia Pictures also refused to distribute the film, which forced the producers to purchase back the rights and release it by other means. Part of the reason for Columbia balking at distribution was that by the time the 150 hours of footage had been whittled into a two-hour film there was widespread desire amongst Americans to put the war behind them. What Kopkind referred to as "post-war cynicism and movement fatigue" thus hampered the film's distribution.

Kopkind concluded by urging readers to see the film that he hoped "might provoke a resurgence of attention to the unexamined questions of the 'Vietnam era.'"[96]

---

[96] Ibid, p. 44.

EPILOGUE

The Vietnam War was a primary focus of the editorial staff at *Ramparts Magazine* during the 1960s and early 1970s. The war and the civil rights movement seemed to be the very lifeblood of the magazine. *Ramparts* published more essays about Vietnam than about any other single topic. Chapters in this book thus highlighted the magazine's articulation of Vietnam as several wars in one, including as a cultural phenomenon and abstraction. Subsequent chapters examined the magazine's depiction of corporate interests in America's war in Indochina, followed by a chapter that examined Washington's war in Vietnam. That chapter was followed by an examination of the war lived by American soldiers, as well as the war the Vietnamese people endured. Writers and editors at *Ramparts*, as chapter four articulated, spent a great deal of ink humanizing both American combatants and the Vietnamese people, which was in stark contrast to the abstract, callous, and dehumanizing depiction of dead combatants (and civilians) as "body count," that was obscenely prevalent amongst the mainstream American media. The final chapter of this book examined *Ramparts Magazine's* unflinching advocacy of the antiwar movement in the U.S., which lost a great deal of momentum in the decades after the end of the Vietnam War.

www.ingramcontent.com/pod-product-compliance
Lightning Source LLC
Chambersburg PA
CBHW061824040426
42447CB00012B/2799